To Tammy,

Enjoy the read. Hope it's helpful!

AGAINST HER WILL

BY JOHN HOWARD WYMAN

Against Her Will - A Cautionary Tale
Author John Howard Wyman
First Edition

Published by John Howard Wyman
ISBN: 978-0-9848551-0-0

Cover Design by Bret Cook | Book Layout by Impressions Design
Printed in the USA

TO ORDER AGAINST HER WILL:

www.Amazon.com
JohnHowardWyman@gmail.com
970-948-5408

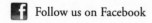 Follow us on Facebook

This book is dedicated to Howard Eldon Wyman, who gave me strength, courage, and compassion, and taught me how to be a man.

And Grandma Teacher, who taught me caring, humility, how not to be judgmental, and to be a human being.

ACKNOWLEDGEMENTS

I'd like to thank my girlfriend Robin, who stayed the course with me, even when she realized my family was too dysfunctional to make the Jerry Springer Show.

My brother Bill, for helping Mom get to Colorado to heal, My mother for her self-determination to escape. Deb, for being a guardian angel, and my editor, Joy, without whom this book would not have been possible.

CONTENTS

PART I

PART II

PART III

PART I

CHAPTER I
THE SKULL

I held the skull in my hand as I sat shoulder to shoulder with my brother Bill. It was dirty, with the lower jaw missing. It had few teeth left, and as I gazed at it, I thought to myself, "This is not an infant's," but it didn't seem as large as my head. I knew it was real because it reminded me of the chicken bones I'd bitten into while growing up. I looked over to my brother, not saying a word, and crawled out from underneath the front porch of our family home where I'd lived since I was five years old. It was muddy and wet under the porch, but my brother and I played there often.

I hurried to the side door of the house, went in, and called for my dad. He came down to the basement landing immediately, and I handed him the skull. He looked at it and then at me and I said, "Dad, can I take it to school for show and tell?" He looked at me and without hesitating, said, "No, son, you can't." I didn't question his authority because Dad's word was law. I was nine years old.

So, as boys will be boys, Bill and I went about our business, playing for the rest of that wet spring afternoon, not giving much thought to what we'd discovered. We were then ignorant of what lay ahead for us, and of the fact that the summer of that year would change our lives forever.

My mom was pregnant with her sixth child during that summer of '64. We'd been told that one child was stillborn in 1960. It was a baby girl, and even though she had never breathed, she had a name, Nancy Sue. A fleeting thought went through my mind; could that have been her skull? Could she have lived long enough to develop teeth? Why would they have hidden her? These thoughts, though fleeting, were troubling.

That summer of '64 was marked by many unusual happenings. When school let out for vacation, I was abruptly sent to live with my paternal grandparents. There I had no friends or siblings to play with, only these older people who I assumed loved me, but with whom I had spent very little time. Gram and Gramps were very good to me. They rarely raised their voices and never raised a hand to me. I got to go with Gramps to his stockyards or the farm and he always saved some chores to keep me occupied. This was more freedom that I'd ever experienced. The summer, though, did go by slowly.

This rhythm was broken, however, one evening as we watched TV A phone call informed us that Mom had given birth to a baby boy, on the same day of the United States' first unmanned lunar landing, July 31, 1964. I don't think I'll ever forget that day.

I thought I'd be going home soon after the birth of the baby, but that didn't happen for another three weeks or so. I didn't mind because my grandparents didn't yell or hit me for wetting the bed and that seemed so foreign to me. They just put a waterproof cover on the bed. They were this kind and thoughtful throughout my life and I would spend more and more time with them. I loved them till the day they died and I knew I was their favorite.

I went home a few days before school started, happy to see my friends, family, and my new baby brother. I had all but forgotten about the skull I found earlier that spring. Maybe that's why I was sent away. I'll never know.

I didn't think of the skull again until my sixteenth summer. My parents also owned the house next to 1035 North Winnebago Street, where I'd made my unusual find. 1031 was an art and ceramics studio with bedrooms upstairs where I'd lived with my oldest brother Marc from the time I was thirteen. I guess my parents had had enough of me by that age, so they put me under the roof next door. I had a lot more freedom, but I still was beaten and the neighborhood was turning into the hood.

I'd just finished painting the inside of 1031 when someone fucked up the air ducts for the furnace and blew black soot everywhere. So now it was up to me to clean it, and it took weeks. What a job. While I was taking a cigarette break one day, I looked out the window of 1031 to see my father and brother-in-law tearing off the front stairs of 1035. I didn't think anything was odd until they poured the footers for the new stairs. They poured enough cement for a new walkway, but they didn't stop there. It ended up being a six-feet by ten-feet slab under the stairs and porch, and this was a huge porch.

I thought about that skull again for a few days, but figured it was just a coincidence. Besides, at that age there were other things on my mind: girls, getting high, music, friends and other teen-age concerns.

It was another thirty years or so before I would talk about the skull again. I remember it very well. My paternal grandfather and I were on one of our cross-country trips from Chicago to Texas to attend his last sheep industry leadership school. Gramps was one of the foremost leaders in the sheep industry. In his day, he'd testified before the U.S. Congress, started the sheep industry leadership school, and prevented ranchers from using poison collars on sheep to control coyotes and other predators. He basically ran the industry and his word was gold.

On our return trip from Texas, we talked about everything from politics and money to Native Americans, relationships, and life in general. Somewhere in the Oklahoma panhandle, after what we agreed was the worst meal on our travels, we started to converse about my home life and upbringing. Even though Gramps knew my father ruled with an iron fist and had a very short temper, when I told him about all the beatings I'd received, and his violent rages directed at me at least five times more than at my siblings, he was appalled. He couldn't understand because he hadn't brought Dad up that way. Gramps was a big Kansas farm boy, Army Air Corp. drill instructor, and strong as a bull, but said he'd only spanked Dad once, and felt terrible about it. He just couldn't comprehend his son's behavior.

As our conversation progressed, I finally brought up the subject of the skull by saying, "Gramps, what I'm about to tell you I've kept to myself for years. Just before that summer I spent with you and Gramma, I found a human skull under the house at 1035 and took it to Dad. When I asked him if I could take it to school, he told me I couldn't." Gramps looked at me in disbelief for a moment, but I know he could tell I was being truthful. He was silent for a few minutes and then asked me very seriously what I thought I should do.

I thought for only a second and said, "Gramps, I think he'll just have to live with it and take the mystery to his grave. It's been so long anyway, and he'll have to answer to his maker."

It took until May of 2009 for me to finally get this off my chest and call the local police department in Rockford, Illinois. They sent an officer to my brother Bill's house to interview me. He wasn't a detective, but a black cop K-9 patrol. He questioned me first and I repeated the story as best as I could recall and even showed him where I had discovered the skull.

Next, he questioned my brother Bill while I stood on the stairs and listened. Bill reconfirmed my story but added some details that brought me back to that day some forty years ago. Specifically, he added that he never touched the skull. Of course he hadn't; it was my find, my snake, my arrowhead, and at that age, I wasn't about to share it with him.

The officer took notes and said something to the effect that I was just doing this to get back at my dad for filing an order of protection against me, my brother, and half his grandchildren. I guess he didn't believe me, so the very next day I went downtown to the FBI office.

While most people would be apprehensive about such an encounter, I wasn't. I just walked into the building and up the elevator to the most secured and intimidating door I'd ever seen. Not bothered in the least, I just rang the buzzer and asked to talk to an agent. Since I had just left a court hearing, I looked every bit a lawyer in my faux Armani suit and short haircut. An agent who was a little younger than I and more casually dressed answered the door and introduced himself as Randy. He invited me to sit down and asked me what was on my mind. I told him it was an old story and described the situation with my father. I told him I had already talked to the local police but felt I should tell a higher authority.

We sat out in the waiting room, never going through the intimidating steel door. We were opposite each other with a chair between us. I felt relaxed and at ease in this casual setting. The conversation was very direct and to the point. He'd ask a few questions, and I'd answer as accurately as I could. This went on for about twenty minutes.

After the interview, he told me he was very busy at the time, but he would keep the case in his files for a later investigation which would include cadaver dogs that could smell bone that was 100 years old. Before thanking Randy for his time, I asked him one more question. "Do you believe me?" And he responded with a very positive "yes." I then asked him why.

Randy explained that he was highly trained in interrogation and used his techniques of observing body language, eye contact and voice fluctuations to determine that I was telling the truth. We said our goodbyes and he told me again he'd look into it and to keep in touch.

I rolled out of the building feeling total vindication. The huge weight of that burden was finally off my chest, and, "Oh, what a feeling!"

CHAPTER II
LET THE BEATINGS BEGIN!

I don't really recall my first spankings. I'm sure they were little swats on the rear, the usual vacation roadside spanking. Except for the fact that I was a bed wetter until I was thirteen years old. Many times I was yanked out of bed in the middle of the night and forced to try to pee. If I wet the bed, I was often spanked while I was half asleep. As I got older, it got worse.

I was often thrown into the bathtub and made to sleep in my urine-soaked blankets for the rest of the night. I was scared to death as the centipedes crawled around in the wet darkness, and I'd cry myself to sleep. My parents would also hang my dirty sheets out of my window for the neighbor kids to see. It was very humiliating. My brother and sister nicknamed me "Piss a Rooster" and threatened to tell the neighborhood kids; that was also hurtful and cruel. It made me tough, though, and I learned very young not to take things personally, to just roll with the punches. I quit wetting the bed at thirteen.

The first beatings I remember were administered by my mother. I don't remember why I was getting whipped, but Mom would make me go to the lilac bush and bring back a switch from it. Then I had to peel the bark off. Then she would go about whipping my lower extremities till I had welts everywhere. It hurt like hell, and the welts would stay for at least a week.

I remember Dad's beatings began shortly thereafter. He wouldn't use a switch, but his leather dress belt. I still can't recall why, but I'm sure I did something that really pissed him off. The belt left huge welts and bruises, and sometimes he'd draw blood. By this time, at age 12 or 13, I don't remember any of my friends being treated that way at home. They'd know when I was in trouble, and make a quick exit.

The two most severe beatings were done by both my parents. The first was when I didn't deliver my Goldblatts' circulars. Mom caught me putting most of them in a dumpster. When I got home and lied about it, she bent me over the piano bench, sat all 350 pounds of herself on me and started beating with one of the rolled up papers. I was thrashing and kicking my feet, when our German shepherd took a hold of my leg and ripped a chunk of meat out of it all the way to the bone.

By the time my mom became aware of what had happened, there was blood everywhere, and she panicked, realizing she had crossed the line. She put me up in her bed, propped my leg up and waited at least two hours until Dad came home.

I knew it was bad, but didn't know how bad. I don't know what was discussed, but they took me to the E.R. and it took over 60 stitches to sew me up. To this day I still carry that scar, and my foot is still numb.

The next beating I remember was the most horrific of my young life. My brother Bill and I were doing dishes and were fucking with each other when it got out of hand. He threw a knife at me but missed. So I threw a spoon back at him, hitting him in the back of his head. The spoon stuck for a moment, then dropped to the floor. Bill was screaming and blood was gushing everywhere. Dad ran up from the basement, pushed me away, took care of Bill, and sent me to my room.

It must've been about 40 minutes when he came upstairs. He started to hit me, but I fought back. He yelled for my older brother Marc and when he appeared, my sister's boyfriend Greg was with him. The two older boys grabbed me and held me over the dirty toilet. Dad, still very angry, proceeded to shave every hair off my head, while I fought and struggled. But my father wasn't done yet.

As I think back now, I can't even imagine someone holding on to that rage and anger for such a long time. My father dragged me from that filthy bathroom, and I still had enough strength to try to resist. When he finally got me to my older brother's bedroom, he threw me on the single bed and pinned my shoulders with his knees. He then commenced to give me the worst beating I had yet endured. He weighed about 220 pounds and outweighed me by about 100 pounds. The beating seemed to go on forever, and, in retrospect, I feel I must have had an out-of-body experience.

As my father knelt over me, the full weight of his body on my shoulders, he went into a frenzy. Open-handed, right and left, he pummeled my face, like a golfer hitting a driver as hard as possible, with lefts and rights as my head snapped back and forth, never letting up. This went on for at least fifteen minutes, with me screaming, crying, and begging him to stop. No one attempted to stop him; I don't even know if they watched.

When he finally exhausted his energy he stopped and left. I was alone, sobbing so hard, I was literally sucking air. Once I regained my sense of reality, and able to breathe normally, I had this burning sensation as if my face was on fire. Sometimes the body has its own way of shutting down pain.

This happened about four days before Christmas. I

was grounded, not allowed to see any friends, and kept out of school. Again, I didn't realize until later in life that they had sequestered me for three and a half weeks, at first because my face was swollen and then because of the bruising. You could actually see imprints of my father's hands imbedded in my face for about four weeks.

When I was finally able to go back to school, I wore a Jack Nicholson <u>Cuckoo's Nest</u> blue knit stocking hat to try to cover my bald head. I think my best friend's parents and some of my teachers had some idea that something had happened, but no one spoke up.

After that beating, I don't recall my father beating me for a long time. But something must have happened shortly after I turned 15, early in my sophomore year of high school. By then my neighborhood had turned from poor white trash to pretty much a black hood. Having grown up in a grade school that was predominantly black, I had plenty of fights in fifth and sixth grade. I didn't want to fight, but my father became extremely racist, as were the parents of my black friends. We all still wanted to play like kids should, and to this day I still keep in contact with them.

Back to my sophomore year; Dad came at me again. We had open campus and school hours were scattered, which wasn't structured enough for me. I'd skip classes that didn't appeal to me. I would only go to art and English classes, and was already an accomplished potter. That year I probably got into some sort of trouble for skipping classes, and my father tried to go off on me again, except this time I was much bigger and stronger. I ran away and made my first escape at only fifteen years of age.

I took off with two kids from school, a white girl and a black kid. I don't recall their names or even why they were running away, but we panhandled for money, got bus tickets, and off we went on a Greyhound. I'm not sure why, but we headed for St. Louis, Missouri. I remember being nervous at the bus station in Rockford because my mom's stepfather worked for them, but once we were on the bus, my fear went away. It was a long trip since we stopped in every little town along the way. I stayed awake most of the time, worried that the police were looking for us, but we made it.

Among the three of us, we had very little money left. As we tried to figure out how to get some, we were approached by a man between 30 and 40 years old. He made a proposition, but only to me. Being a street kid, I had some inkling of what he wanted. Being broke and tired, I decided to go with him anyway.

He drove to East St. Louis to an industrial area, ending up in an apartment above a warehouse. This man offered me $100 to blow me. I said, "I'm straight, but for $100 I'll let ya. But you stink, so go take a shower first." As soon as I heard him get into the shower I pushed his heavy dresser across the door, grabbed his wallet, and made a quick exit.

As I was running at what felt like the speed of light, I relieved his wallet of what cash it held and tossed it to the ground, never breaking stride. Somehow I managed to hitch a ride with someone who told me I was in the worst part of the city for a white boy. He was right; the area made my hood look like Kiddieland!

I made my way back to the bus station, looking for my friends. I found the two of them sleeping on the floor. Finally feeling safe once again, I counted my money. It was a good haul, about $300, probably the most money I'd had at any time in my life. I stashed a hundred dollar bill in the fifth pocket of my jeans and told my friends I had $150 and change for us to go on. I don't think I told my friends how I got the money. I guess I felt kind of guilty. I'd never stolen anything like that before, or since, except maybe pocket change from Ma. But that's survival!

We stayed at the rundown Warwick Hotel for a couple of days, trying to figure out what to do next. I think my friends thought they were on some sort of honeymoon, not getting out of bed much, so I decided to take off on my own. After hopping a city bus, I ended up in University City. I hooked up with some twenty-year-old hippies who let me stay on their floor.

They got me a job at the old Fox Theater, cleaning up after Grateful Dead concerts at night. During the day, we'd go to an underground printing shop and silkscreen "Free Angela Davis" posters and then go post them on walls and telephone poles. The hippies were very kind to me. They fed me and gave me a safe roof over my head, with no fear of getting beaten. .With the exception of the cockroaches everywhere, I felt pretty darn safe.

After about two weeks, I sent a letter to my friend Andy. I think his parents intercepted it and gave it to my school, so everyone was looking for me. Since I still had money left, I said my goodbyes to my hippie friends, got a bus ticket, and headed back to Rockford, not home, but to Grandma's house. I wasn't about to be beaten by my father ever again.

Grandma must have brokered a hell of a deal, because I got to go back home for another year and then some without a beating, but that would change halfway through my junior year.

We still had a lot of racial tension in school with armed guards in the hallways. It wasn't an ideal learning environment, to say the least. I got in my last fight in school and the last at home, all in the same day. After the fight at school, I was finally expelled from the school system, all nine high schools. When I got in trouble in school, my parents never went to conferences, so I'd just serve the suspensions and go back when the time was up. But this time it was for good.

My father was outraged. He said that because of my situation, the family's car insurance had been cancelled. He told me to leave his fuckin' house immediately. I'm sure I was defiant at this point, and probably lipped off. Whatever it was, I saw that all-too-familiar look I'd known most of my life appear on my dad's face, and it wasn't pretty.

Now I wasn't one of those kids who bragged about taking out their dads who were drunk, because my father didn't drink. He was just plain evil. That in itself took me a long time to come to grips with. He was educated, smart, and pretty normal on the outside. He hid his real self behind those attributes.

That night his real self came out swinging. He threw fists left and right, as hard as he could. But this night would be very different. Those punches would never land. I'd morphed into a man/boy at six feet tall and 165 pounds. Well-muscled and mean, I knew how to fight, but I never hit my dad that night. I didn't have to. Every time he'd throw a punch and swing a fist, I either caught it or dodged it. This went on for about ten minutes or so, till he'd strained or wore out every muscle in his body.

As a last resort, he wrestled me to the floor, but it took more than he had to restrain me. It also took my mother and younger brother Bill. Once my parents held me secure on the floor, Dad told Bill to get the dog's chain off the front porch. When he came back, Dad took the chain and tried to tie my legs up while Mom sat on me. The chain cut into my ankles and I struggled. It drew blood, but didn't seem to hurt.

Dad then went to call the police to come get me and take me to juvenile hall. Somehow I managed to squeeze out from underneath Mom, tear off those chains and hit the front door, escaping, never looking back.

I went to Grandma's house and never lived under the same roof with that man again. We eventually patched up our relationship, but it took a long time. From that day forward, I realized that evil does exist.

CHAPTER III

THE AFFAIRS

The first affair I remember was one my father had with the neighbor across the street from us. Her name was Mariann G. The way we kids discovered this was at the family dinner table.

We always ate in the kitchen at a large Formica-topped table, with a lip all the way around underneath to hide food we didn't like. There we were, two kids on each side and Dad at the head of the table. Mom was at the other end by the stove, so she could retrieve food faster. At some point, Mom got up and took the Pyrex coffee pot that was percolating and walked down to Dad to pour his coffee. Instead of pouring the coffee into the cup, though, she poured it directly on his crotch. Then all hell broke loose. Mom was yelling, and it didn't take long to figure out why she was mad and why her anger extended across the street to Mariann.

Dad turned to Mom, and before she could hasten a retreat, he punched her square in the mouth. Mom didn't go down, but when she turned toward the table, she sported the biggest fat lip I'd ever seen, blood running down her chin. I'm sure he loosened a few teeth.

By then my older brother Marc, who was about 16, lunged toward Dad as he got up and ran out the back door. By the time the rest of us kids got outside to see what was happening, Marc had Dad bent backward over the convertible Karmann Ghia. Marc was holding a long metal pole we used to chip ice like he was going to take a swing. He threatened Dad, saying, "Don't you ever hit my mother again!" For the first time, Dad was scared, and I saw fear in his face. After Mom's pleading, Marc finally let him up. Dad took off and ran and I didn't see him for a couple of days. I don't think he used that cock again for a long time, except to piss.

The next time he went over the fence was probably after he healed. He came home from work unusually early one day. One of his coworkers, Bob, had jumped him at work. Bob was a big football player type, so it didn't take much for him to take Dad out. He was in bed for a few days, nursing his beat-up body. We kids then found out that Dad had a thing for Bob's wife Linda, and I guess he took it too far. Their friendship broke up, and we didn't do anything with their family anymore. We all lost on that one; we would never play with their kids again.

A few years later, Bob got promoted over my father. Eventually Bob fired him, and I'm sure the affair had something to do with it. My dad was fifty-something at the time, and he never held a steady job as a mechanical engineer again.

The last affair I was aware of came about many years later when Dad asked to use my house for a noon business meeting. Since I wasn't very close to my parents, they didn't have a key to my place, and Dad's request seemed somewhat out of order. I finally gave in, though, because Dad seemed desperate. I thought all must have gone well when Dad brought the key back to my hair salon, thanked me, and went on his way.

I finished up my normal nine to eleven hour day at work and, as usual, went out to dinner and drinks. When I arrived at home at about nine that night, everything appeared to be in place. As usual, I shucked off my clothes, took a hit off my pot pipe and went out to a relaxing sit in the hot tub. After half an hour or so, I got out of the tub before wrinkled skin set in, took my shower, put on my robe, and went to my bedroom to relax and wait for one of my girlfriends to come over. The bed was made so I grabbed a book, took off my robe, pulled the covers back, and plopped my body right in the middle of the bed. I must have jumped three feet in the air, almost hitting the ceiling fan.

My father had left his calling card, a wet spot in the center of the bed. I was so pissed off I'm sure I used every vulgarity known to man. Not only had he gone into my room, he had no qualms about using his own son's bed for his "business meeting," and had the nerve not to change the sheets. It was just wrong, so wrong. No son should have to roll in his father's mess.

I took another shower, changed the sheets, and tried to call him. He wouldn't answer. When I finally did catch up with Dad, I gave him an ass-chewing he wouldn't soon forget. And he never used my house again as long as I lived there. I never did tell Mom, but looking back now, I probably should have.

It was wrong, so very wrong!

CHAPTER IV

WHAT WAS GOOD

Believe it or not, there were some good things my parents gave me, some genetically and some environmentally. Gene-wise, both my parents were very good looking. Mom had modeled some when she was younger, but with time she had become very overweight. Dad had very dark curly hair and eyes so brown they were almost black, which probably came from his Native American heritage and not so much from his Norwegian side. They were both very tall, so I ended up being 6'4".

Artistically, my mother was good at almost everything she did, ceramics, sculpting, painting, stained glass, etc. On the other hand, Dad was an engineer, tool and die maker, mechanic, and could fix anything. With Dad, we would learn to take a VW engine out of the micro bus, take it apart, clean it on the kitchen table (Dad was meticulous about some things), put it back together and back in the car over a weekend.

Dad would get extremely angry when we'd use his torque wrench to knock off lug nuts, or his ratchet wrench for a hammer. For that I'm sure we got whupped! But by the time I was 14, I could make things from wood, metal, plastic, or just about anything.

Mom, however, would give all of us some artistic talent of some form, art, music, or almost anything creative. I would go on to become an accomplished potter and sculptor, winning awards. Twice, I was a state champion in hairdressing, a career at which I became very successful at an extremely young age. It was also the career all my siblings chose to follow and used as a stepping stone in life.

We also acquired a great love for classical and jazz music. We'd go to the symphony orchestra every Friday night during the summer, run around, play, and listen to music. I remember these evenings as pleasant times.

Because we couldn't afford normal vacations, from the time I can remember we went camping. I'm talking six people in a V-Dub Bus, traveling all over Wisconsin, but mostly in Door County. We'd beach camp on Lake Michigan, camp in the forest, and explore areas that were very different from our life in the hood. I learned about everything you could do in the wilderness, setting up camp, cooking, K.P., and socializing with other campers.

With the exception of the long car rides to get to our destination, which were nauseating because Dad chain-smoked in the car, and the occasional vacation roadside spankings, I recall these experiences as things that were good!

CHAPTER V
THE GRAND REFUGE

During my turbulent upbringing, I figured out early about survival skills and discovered my grand refuge, my grandparents' homes, maternal and paternal. Someone must've been watching out for me because I was bestowed with four of the most unusual, but very caring and loving grandparents.

First and foremost was my Grandma "Teacher." She earned the name "Teacher" because she was one, in every aspect of the word. She was a southern lady, a coal miner's daughter. At eighteen, she started teaching in a two-room school house in southern Illinois where her mother was the principal.

I've heard and read stories of her first year of teaching when she scooted all the school children into the storm cellar just before the tornado hit and saved their lives. More than six hundred died that day, but not the kids on her watch. That was Grandma "T."

She was also the most nonjudgmental person I've ever met. For instance, her mother, my great-grandmother, was also a teacher and from the South. She used to damn the niggers and praise God all in one breath, with her hand on the Bible. I couldn't believe my grandma was her daughter, because when Grandma "T" moved north, she ended up teaching in a predominantly black school. She loved her students and they loved her and stayed in contact with her throughout their lives. She was a very special human being.

Growing up from age 12 to 17, while I was still living with or by my parents, I knew there was a safe place for me to go if need be. Besides her full-time teaching, Grandma was a wife to Gramps, and took care of her elderly mother. During the school week, she only slept from 2 a.m. to 5 a.m. I'm not sure how she did all this without drugs, but she did. No matter what time of day it was, though, she was always there for me. She lived six blocks away, and I'd run there often, either after or to prevent a beating from my dad. He couldn't do that there, not in her house. To say the least, she was the most influential human in shaping my life.

She left her husband after catching him with her best friend. Her second husband treated us grand-kids as if we were his own flesh and blood. Early on he'd take us to church every Sunday. He was a kind man from Boston. He had a very distinct waddle in his walk, and we'd make fun at him behind his back, but never maliciously.

As I became older, he'd drive me to work or beauty school if I asked. Being a dirty old man, if my girlfriends were around, he'd always try to get them to sit on his lap. It was an ongoing joke with us and with my girls. On occasion, he'd be taking me to school or my job, and he'd try to shock me by asking if I was "getting any." All in all, with his good sense of humor, he inspired me to love women even more.

Then there's Grandpa Howard. I'll try not to hold back in my writing, but I have to save some of him for my next book. He was truly a Renaissance man in every sense of the word. To begin with, he was your typical Kansas farm boy. He had short legs and a long upper torso, and was as strong as could be. He was kind of like the first generation who walked upright, but with a genius I.Q. He was pretty much "the Don" of the sheep industry. He was an Army Air Corps drill instructor and stenographer. After the war, he finished college in a year and a half at the University of Illinois with a master's degree in business.

Later in life, he went on to become an actor, writer, and artist, producing a small, but good body of work. Above all, Grandpa was my mentor, teacher, friend, and my courage. I spent four or five summers with him and Grandma. I was the only child in my family to do this and was later to find out that these stays were for discipline purposes. But neither he nor Grandma ever hit me, and only Grandma yelled at me. That was just the natural, funny way she had of communicating with the men she loved.

When they would return me at the end of the summer, they'd always tell my parents the same thing. "If you keep John busy solving problems, whether on the farm or at the stock yards, he's never a problem." They didn't even punish me for wetting the bed. How nice!

The most important lessons I learned from Gramps were to have compassion for others, to believe in yourself, to stick with your convictions to the very end, and to always be truthful.

This brings me to one of the most important parts of my story. Gramps was ten years younger than Grandma. He met her when my dad invited him over. Dad was eleven, Gramps was twenty-one, and Grandma was thirty-one at the time. Gramps rented a room in Grandma's boarding house, and my dad took a liking to him. At the time he was an Army Air Corps D.I, and Dad didn't have a proper father. That's how the two of them hooked up.

Grandma, being ten years older, may have been the original "cougar," but somehow I doubt that. Gramps always justified their age difference by saying, "Ya know, all my brothers passed early from heart attacks, so I'll be pushing up flowers before her."

But that was not to be. As she grew older, Grandma's health problems started earlier than expected. She had bad knees, so in her early sixties she needed a wheel chair to get around, but it didn't slow her down in the least. That was until she had her first stroke, and later on, she experienced memory loss, delusions, and lost the ability to take in nourishment orally.

Before all this happened, however, I asked her a question I'd asked numerous times before. "Who was my biological grandfather?" In 1967, when I was 12, my older brother Marc had told me Howard Wyman wasn't my real grandfather, but that a mysterious author was my real grandfather. Marc showed me this at the local library by showing me my real grandfather's obituary in the 1967 World Book Encyclopedia. I was crushed, to say the least. I never brought it up much, but when I did, Grandma would change the subject or distract me. She just wouldn't talk about him. By the time she finally got around to telling me, I'd studied all I could about him and discovered he may have been the most prolific writer of the last century.

I'll never forget the incident when Grandma finally spilled all the beans. It occurred one summer day while I was visiting her and Gramps at their small farm in Bristol, Illinois. Even after I moved to Aspen, I would spend time there working as a farmhand. That's when I'd trade in my scissors and surrender my baby soft hands, of which I'm still very proud, to become a lumberjack and a chain saw Tasmanian devil down in the swampy part of his farm. I'd be literally breathing in mosquitoes and beating the hell out of my body for eight days.

On this particular day, I came into the house to cool

down and have lunch. My persistent questioning had finally gotten to Grandma, and she agreed to quell my curiosity about my grandfather, but with stipulations. The first stipulation was that during the complete disclosure on this matter, Grandpa Howard would be in the room. At that time I found this odd and wondered if this would be hurtful for him, but Grandma made the rules. The second condition was that I'd never ask these questions again and would not talk about it in her presence. This seemed fair, and like I said, she made the rules.

Grandma sat across from me in her wheelchair at the small kitchen table at which we'd just eaten, and Gramps paced the kitchen somewhat nervously, doing dishes and whatnot. When Grandma finally started to speak, my eyes must've been as large as saucers, like a little boy seeing his first lamb being born, as she spoke. She didn't beat around the bush, but was direct and to the point.

Grandma explained that when she was twenty years old, she went to work for a major movie studio as a proof reader for scripts. She met a man who claimed to be a ghost writer for a famous author. He went by the name Eugene Francisco Valté. She said she was smitten by him and a romance developed. Shortly thereafter they married.

Grandma didn't elaborate on their home life or marriage, only saying that she ended up bearing his child, my father. Later, the marriage was dissolved and considered illegal due to the fact that the author Valté was married to another woman in the same city and had fathered another child six months earlier. When Grandma discovered this, I'm sure she went ballistic in her own way since she was half Cherokee and half Scotch Irish. "Oh, to have been a fly on the wall," I thought to myself.

After being found out by two very angry young women,

Valté headed south of the border, adding two more aliases to the twenty-nine he already had. He never returned to the United States again, unless he did so under another name. He went on to pen quite a few more novels, at least eight of which were made into movies. I probably picked up my womanizing genes from him, except I never married. I hope and pray I pick up a small part of his writing abilities; that's the least he could have left me.

When Grandma finished her story, she simply wheeled herself out of the room. It was then that I realized Grandpa was still in the room. Not saying a word, I grabbed my hat and gloves and headed back to Mosquito Alley, chain saw in hand.

A few months after my conversation with Grandma, she suffered a severe stroke, which paralyzed one side of her body and weakened the other. Timing is everything, and I believe nothing happens by chance. I'm thankful I asked her again when I did.

After her stroke, Grandpa stood steadfast, and I was back in school, learning compassion, sacrifice, and courage. Grandma needed to be fed, bathed, etc., but Grandpa didn't warehouse her by sending her to a nursing home. He showed great strength and love in his care of her. Grandma had lost her ability to swallow, among other things. Since Gramps worked out of home, he tried his best for the next three years, going as far as to puree her food, but she couldn't keep it down. So Gramps, being as bright as he was, started feeding Grandma baby food. It worked perfectly and because of this, her doctor had this procedure published in the Journal of American Medicine. Baby food has become a standard for stroke victims since then. By the way, the doctor took the credit for this innovation.

On one of my pilgrimages to the farm, I would also

have the opportunity to spoon feed Grandma. She would cry because she was still cognizant of her situation, but I'd have none of that, and reassured her she'd probably done the same for me when I was an infant. Those words always put her at ease and made her smile.

Over the next year or so, Grandma's physical condition deteriorated to the point that she had to be tube fed. Since Grandma was a forward thinking person at the time, she put in her health directives that she didn't want to starve to death. But when she drafted this document, tube feeding hadn't been developed. I'm sure she would have ruled it out for herself.

During the end of her life, Grandma started having hallucinations. I remember one incident when my sister and I were at the end of her bed and Grandma pointed to the ceiling corner and said, "Can you see the helicopter?"

My sister immediately snapped at her, saying, "There are no helicopters in the corner. You're seeing things."

To which, without hesitation, I piped in, "Grandma, just because I can't see it doesn't mean it's not there." Who was I to say?

During the rest of her time with us, I even helped Gramps bathe her. It was awkward for a millisecond, but I soon realized I was back in school, Grandpa's school. And what I found most fascinating about the process of passing was during bathing, seeing her skin become smoother, almost translucent. It was a beautiful experience, almost like going back to the womb. After Grandma passed, I still went back to the farm to help Gramps. Even with their age difference, he would tell me he was blessed with 49 years of marriage to her.

On what was to be my final trip to the farm while Gramps was still with us, we were cleaning out one of his many buildings when we came across 100 or so of Grandma's tube feeding boxes. I made the call to take them to the burn pile and while loading the boxes in the pick-up, Gramps stopped and asked me if I thought he did the right thing by using that method of keeping Grandma alive. I simply put my hand on Gramps' shoulder and said, "Gramps, you did the right thing at the time." Gramps and I got a lot of things done on the farm that week, not knowing it would be the last time we'd see each other in this life.

As I packed my car and prepared to leave, Gramps and I were talking in the driveway. I went to give him a final hug, and afterwards, he looked me in the eye and said, "John, when you quit smoking, you'll be the perfect man." Coming from Gramps, it's possibly the highest compliment I've ever received from anyone.

In December of that same year Gramps passed in his sleep. How beautiful. Even in death he always did everything right. I wrote and read his eulogy at his service. My girlfriend was amazed I could stand in front of a crowd and read it. I said, "It's easy when you know true compassion and true love."

CHAPTER VI
MY GREAT ESCAPE

My great escape began halfway through my junior year of high school in 1972. After getting thrown out of the school system for fighting and trying to evade my father who was trying to beat me, I escaped to Grandma Teacher's. Thank God, or whomever, for Grandma. She gave me a safe haven and a chance in life!

I moved into Grandma's attic room, which was long and not very wide. In fact, at 6'1", I couldn't stand fully erect, but it was a safe room. Grandma had rules and boundaries, but they were very simple-- come home at night, keep a job, and think about my future, all of which I did before moving on to my first apartment.

I had a job working in produce in a local Italian supermarket, Logli's. While working there, I tried to join the Navy. I went to the recruiting center, scored high on all the tests, but had to have my parents' signatures. They wouldn't sign for me, and at the time, I thought it was their way of controlling me until I was 18. But looking back now, maybe, just maybe, they were doing me a final favor because the Viet Nam War was still going on.

Next, my parents thought I'd make a good potter's apprentice since I was already an accomplished potter. They knew of a studio in Wisconsin that might work out, but I had different dreams at the time. I was involved with my first serious "puppy love."

It happened when I was 16. I had my tonsils out, and in those days, you stayed in the hospital for a couple of days. While I was there, I fell head over heels for a candy striper named Belinda. She was still in high school and candy stripers were volunteers. We dated for about two months before Belinda went back to her old boy friend.

I was somewhat heartbroken, but every time I'd call her, I'd end up with her twin sister Barbara on the phone, counseling me. After a week or so, Barbara said, "How about me? How about you and I dating?" This seemed like a small gesture, a consolation prize, if you will. Little did I know what a large impact that small gesture would have on my professional life for the next 38 years.

Barbara was going to beauty school for half a day and to high school for the other half. We fell in love and started dating. Barbara was shy and meek, but beautiful, and so in love with me, she didn't want me to go away. She was very persistent, and finally suggested I go to beauty school with her so we could be together. She thought that with my artistic talent for pottery, I'd make a great hairdresser because I was already working in three-dimensional forms. After more persuading and my getting over the fact that all the hairdressers I knew were gay, except for my mother's, I finally succumbed and started beauty school in January of 1972. This little side step in life changed it forever.

I got a job working night shifts at a gas station, checking oil, filling cars up, cleaning windshields, etc. I was working 60 hours a week and going to beauty school 40 hours. That didn't leave much time for anything else, except sleeping, eating, and personal hygiene. I look back now and wonder how I did all that, only to write it off to youth.

Barbara and I would be a couple for about six more months, until she told me about a "funny" uncle who had been molesting her since she was fourteen. We were finally able to confront this situation with a family meeting, but it didn't go so well. Her mother took the uncle's side with a few cock and bull stories that made it look like Barbara's fault. This in itself infuriated me to such a point of anger that her parents sent her away and broke up our relationship. I was heart-broken, but stayed the course and went on to finish beauty school. After finishing school, I would go on to own two hair salons and to become the state of Illinois hairdressing champion twice.

Then, at the age of twenty-one, I'd have another life-changing experience. My brother Marc, an experienced pilot with six hundred hours under his belt, was flying with his instructor on a beautiful Saturday afternoon. He was doing his multi-engine instrument flight rating when he lined up for an instrument approach to the airport. A high-winged plane with an inexperienced pilot came up under his low-winged plane and caused a midair collision. All five people, three in my brother's plane and two in the other plane, died that day. It changed my family dynamics and my life forever. I became the eldest son in the family overnight.

The next few days were a blur. I was a different person after identifying bodies, setting up a funeral, and consoling my family. The thought that gave me the strength to accomplish these things was something my Grandma Donnalee had told me some time before, "Everyone who's supposed to meet will meet." For the first time in my short life, this made sense to me. So keeping my chin up and my composure in place, I was able to make it through this rough time, helping the people who were close to this tragedy.

After the graveside service, everyone left the cemetery but me. Standing there in my good suit, I told the grave digger to take a break, and I grabbed a shovel and proceeded to bury my brother. It was the last thing I could do for him, and it was very healing for me.

Later that day, family and friends all gathered at my house for food, drinks, and to celebrate my brother's life. My father came over to me as I was sitting on the couch, sat next to me crying, and asked if he'd been a good father. I responded without much hesitation that, in fact, he and Mom had given me a great appreciation for art, music, and nature. However, as far as disciplinarians, they had both crossed the line more than a few times, especially when he beat me so severely when I was fourteen that I couldn't go to school for five weeks. I told him I'd forgiven him, but would never forget.

Life went on, but it was different without Marc. Somehow I had changed. Anger, the green monster, and the controlling ways I'd learned from my father suddenly had become part of the past. I finally got those monkeys off my back. I don't, to this day, know why, but what a great feeling it was to be free of those behaviors and to meet relationships, business, and life in general as the new me.

I would be successful in business in Rockford for the next five years. My posse of friends had changed and I started to travel the world with them. One of our men's trips brought us to Aspen, Colorado, which altered my course again. When I returned home from that trip, I'd made up my mind that I wanted to live in Aspen, but it would take another three years for that to come to fruition.

In those three years, however, a lot of things happened. My two brothers and two of my best friends would follow me into the beauty business, with two out of the four making it their life-long career. As for my other friends who were wealthy, they couldn't, for the life of them, figure out why I'd want to give this all up to start over again somewhere else. I'd explain that life's not a dress rehearsal and that the cream always floats to the top. If I was that good at what I did, I'd be okay.

A year before I moved, I stopped by to see how my parents were doing. I hadn't had a lot of contact with them from the time I was seventeen until my brother died when I was twenty-one. The relationship was cautious. I had joined the Masons and the Shriners with my father where we became Shrine clowns, and occasionally my parents came to parties, but that was about the extent of it.

On this day when I pulled up to the house, Dad was lying back with a hand on the stairs and the other on his heart as two black guys with guns chased a white guy down the street. I guess it was a drug deal gone bad. My hood was more dangerous now than ever. Since I was leaving in a year I offered my parents my house to live in while I was on my journey and I'd move back to the hood until I left. They jumped at the offer to live in a middle class neighborhood.

So I lived in the hood for about a year in the house I grew up in, the one with the skull under the front porch. It was quite an experience, since I hadn't spent much time there in nine years. However, I still had parties there, and girlfriends stayed there. It was still the hood, but strangely, I felt safe because I'd grown up there. How safe, I'll never know.

When I was twenty-six, I moved to Aspen. My parents visited me twice in the subsequent eighteen years, and I'd go back to visit once a year. But I'd only see them for about two or three hours each trip, usually for a family dinner, since I was footing the bill. I had become very successful in Aspen.

Life in Aspen was great for about eighteen years until the wheels came off one day, and I lost my house in a poker game. Just kidding. That's not exactly what happened.

But when I was down on my luck, no one was there to catch me, even though several members of my family had followed me to Aspen. I'd cosigned for houses and helped all of them in some way to much better lives than they had back in Rockford, but I received little or no help from them.

After living in my truck for a year with my two dogs, I finally got back on my feet and with the help of my new girlfriend, Robin, was able to purchase a trailer. I still had to file bankruptcy, but that would have meant that my parents would lose my home to live in. Unbeknownst to me, they had forged my signature on my mortgage and had it put in their names.

To save my house in Rockford, I showed my parents how to foreclose the mortgage and keep the house in their name. In doing so, they agreed to two stipulations. One was that they had to sell the house in the hood to my nephew Marc for a dollar, which they did, and the other was to quick claim deed my house back to me after my bankruptcy.

The latter never happened. After my bankruptcy was over, I asked my father to sign my house back over to me. The house was paid for and the ninety thousand in equity would have put me back on my feet fairly quickly.

My father, however, refused, saying that he'd taken care of my house all those years, even though he hadn't made house payments, or paid for insurance or taxes. But he felt it was theirs.

I was upset, to say the least, and our relationship was strained and cautious. I had very little to do with my parents for the next ten years. Can you blame me?

CHAPTER VII

PRISONERS LEFT BEHIND

My two younger brothers and later, I'd realize, my mother, were the prisoners left behind.

Bill, who is two years younger than I, and I were very close growing up and still are today. He used to tag along with my friends and me, and when they weren't there, he was my best friend.

Before my younger brother David was born, Bill was the special child in our family. He was partially deaf and had a learning disability in reading, so was sent to a special summer school camp to learn to read. Bill didn't get the beatings I received, but he got his share, just not as severe as mine. We stayed close as we grew into our teens.

When Bill was about sixteen, I stopped by my parents' house to see him, and I couldn't believe my eyes. There was Bill, sitting on the porch looking at a newspaper. I asked him if he was looking at the pictures, but he said, "Nope, I'm reading." He went on to tell me that the year before, David came home from school one day and was reading. Since David was only seven years old, Bill thought to himself, "I can do that," so he started by forcing himself to read the newspaper every day. He had some basic skills, but looking back now, I think he was probably dyslexic.

I didn't realize much of what was going on at home at

the time because I was living with Grandma Teacher, going to beauty school forty hours a week and working sixty hours a week at the Clark Gas Station on North Main. It was odd, but shortly after I quit working there, the night shift gas station attendant was killed in a robbery, and after working at the Clark station on Auburn Street, shortly before I finished beauty school, the night attendants were executed at that one. But at eighteen years old, I still didn't grasp how vulnerable I was.

Anyway, Bill would go on to father four children with three different women. His first one, Danielle, was born when Bill was only seventeen. He had his second and third children, Mark and Shane, with his long-term girlfriend Kim and his fourth child with his wife Cheryl. The funny thing is that all his children get along, even into adulthood, and treat each other as full siblings. Bill has always loved and cared for his offspring, and never even raised a hand to them.

And then there's David, my youngest brother, who is nine years younger than I. All of us older kids took care of him from the time he was born, since Mom and Dad were busy starting up and running a pottery studio. David was raised like an only child, since he was so much younger than the other siblings. I only remember one incident where my father crossed the line in his discipline. It was shortly after I got my first job as a hairdresser. I was doing Dad's hair at the salon on a Sunday when the shop was closed. David was running around the shop like any nine-year-old would, when I asked him to stop so he wouldn't break anything. As he ran by Dad, he back-handed David and gave him a fat lip and a bloody mouth. For the second time in my life, I stood up to Dad, put my hands firmly on his shoulders and said, "Don't you ever hit him in the head again. If you have to hit him, he has a behind just for that." After that incident, I don't believe he ever touched David again.

As a successful young hairdresser, I had the means to send my little brother to a private high school, with the hope he would get a formal education and be the second college graduate in our family. During his time in high school, I also paid for him to go to beauty school. He finished high school, but didn't go to college right away. He did, however, become a fairly talented hairdresser.

David married young and had four children, but when his kids were young, he cut me off from seeing them. His reason was that I wasn't a born-again Christian. Subsequently, I had very little contact with him or his family. The only news I would receive about him was through the family grapevine, and most of the news I'd get about Dave wasn't good.

Apparently, he was caught with a crack addict prostitute after she kicked out his windshield after servicing him. I can only speculate that he made her do something she didn't want to do. We didn't talk again until Grandpa Howard's funeral, and then it was just cordial. I even went as far as to give him a big hug that day. After that, we had very little contact unless I went back to Gramps' house to help my Aunt Pam, my father's half-sister, which I did every year.

Just before Gramps passed, he told me he was upset with David for taking a tractor and not returning it. It was odd that with Gramps gone, David kind of swept into my Aunt Pam's life, probably because Gramps had left her a modest fortune. David basically moved down to Gramps' farm in December, 2008. I'd later find out the reason was that he was beating his wife Krista and she had filed an order of protection against him. She had to file again in June, 2009.

Knowing that information, I found it hard to believe that Aunt Pam would let him stay with her. Since she had retired, she'd worked extensively with a battered women's shelter. I think Gramps would have been appalled.

I also have a sister, Beth, who is two years older than I. I only remember Beth being physically punished once, when she came home early in her senior year of high school and told Mom and Dad she was pregnant. My mom went absolutely ballistic. She had Beth by her hair and threw her around the front foyer until Dad intervened. That ended up being Beth's escape.

She went on to have two boys, Josh and Andy, but her marriage was cut short when she went over the fence and had an affair with a fellow parishioner at church. But, again, because I wasn't a born-again Christian, she cut me out of her family's life. Later, though, she would follow me out to Aspen to live with me for awhile and work at my salon. She, too, had followed my footsteps into the hair business. Her stay with me lasted about eight months, long enough for her to gain some clientele and for me to help her and her second husband obtain a mortgage on a home near Aspen. It ended when she went out with a friend of mine and didn't come home. Her husband called from Rockford, Illinois, until two in the morning. I couldn't lie, but I really didn't know where she was. This ended our relationship again. All she said to me was, "Even when you're right, I can't stand the sound of your voice."

Beth wasn't at Gramps' funeral, but after the sale of her home near Aspen, she was able to buy a small farm near my brother Dave in Galena, Illinois, and splits her time between there and Aspen. The odd thing is, since Gramps passed, she too has slipped back into my Aunt Pam's life. Funny, isn't it?

PART II

PART II

CHAPTER VIII

HOW DARE HE? WHY WOULD HE? HOW COULD HE?

From what you've read in Part I, I think you've gotten to know me a little, but the next part of the journey I'm about to take you on is the third of my most life changing experiences and reveals the cautionary tale I want to share. The first was meeting Barbara, my "puppy love," which ultimately steered me to my career of the past thirty-eight years. The next one was the death of my oldest brother Marc that showed me that life isn't a dress rehearsal. It's the real deal, so I've tried to follow a path of kindness, love, and compassion in everyday life as much as possible. For me it's been an easier road, and I can say much more pleasant.

The third life-changing experience involves my mother, whom I didn't really care for much. I probably wouldn't even have attended her funeral if she had died before this journey. I loved her for the fact that she brought me into this world, but I really, really, didn't like her.

My story begins in mid-December 2008. I was home for the holidays on the south side of Chicago with my nice Jewish girlfriend Robin and her family. Other than Robin's dad Jerry meeting Gramps before he passed, and her best friend M.C. and brother David meeting the rest of my family at Gramps' funeral, our family hadn't had much contact, so Robin and I went to Gramps' farm to visit my Aunt Pam. Even though Pam owns the farm now, I'll always refer to it as Gramps' since it was his dream house. So I made arrangements for my Brother Bill, his three boys, and Mom and Dad to meet us there.

We arrived early, so it was just Robin, Pam, and I. Those two get along so well that with the exception of my few off-color jokes, I was pretty much left out of the conversation while they started chatting.

About an hour or so after we arrived, I heard the alarm go off for the driveway, announcing someone's arrival. It was Bill, his boys, and Mom and Dad. I video-taped them as they came through the four-car garage, making jokes as I was taping. With a video camera in hand, I couldn't stop myself from giving a running commentary.

After our greeting, we all settled down in the great room to discuss where we would go for brunch. Everything seemed as normal as my family gets. I did a little more video-taping, some of the house, some of the family. I even took one of Gramps' Picassos out of a broken frame so it wouldn't get damaged and documented it too.

As I was video-taping my family, I asked Mom to give me a big toothy grin, but she refused. She had lost a few more front teeth and had a smile like a jack-o'-lantern. I'm sure it bothered her. Since Gramps had cut my father out of his will, I'd talked to Aunt Pam and she assured me that if my parents needed anything, all they had to do was have it fixed and she'd take care of the bill. But she wouldn't just give them cash without a receipt.

After the rendezvous at Gramps', we all went out to brunch at Pam's favorite restaurant. We sat at a large table for eight. Robin sat near Mom, Dad, and Pam, and I sat at the other end with Bill and Goobs, my nephew. Since it was around Christmas, the local high school choir was singing Christmas carols for tips while we ate. After a pleasant brunch, we went back to Gramps' farm, said our goodbyes, and went our separate ways. This would be the last time I'd see my Aunt Pam, who was very close to me.

Robin survived the ordeal because she was aware of my relationship with my parents. On the drive back to her father's house, though, she couldn't avoid asking me about my Mom's teeth. She thought it was disgusting that Pam had promised to take care of them but hadn't had them fixed yet. I assured her that I'd talk with Pam about it, but I never got around to having that conversation with her.

The next time I talked with Pam was the first week of January, 2009. She called me while I was at work. My first reaction was that someone in the family had died because other than a couple of times in my life, I was the one who initiated communications with her.

She had called to tell me that my brother Dave was stressed out trying to get my mother to go to a nursing home because he thought she had early signs of dementia. I assured her I'd call Dave to see if I could help. A few days later I called Dave and we had a lengthy conversation about Mom's condition. He told me that he and Dad had taken Mom to a few doctors who specialized in elder care and that Powell, my dad, was no longer able to care for her. This seemed a bit odd to me at the time because I'd just spent a few hours with Mom and Dad in December and she seemed fine then. I didn't bring this up for whatever reason, but I probably should have.

I had told David I'd help as much as possible, but geographically I was 1,100 miles away. I did talk to Mom, though, and she said she didn't want to leave her home and didn't understand why they were trying to put her away.

I called Dave after my conversation with Mom and told him she sounded o.k. to me, but who was I to say.

Since I hadn't spent much time with Mom and Dad over the previous twenty-eight years, I really wasn't sure how she was. David went on to say that he thought that he and Dad could handle this themselves. I wouldn't hear from Dave again until April, 2009.

Finally, all hell broke loose on April 3, 2009. In the middle of the night I received a frantic phone call from my brother Bill saying there was an incident at my parents' house during which Mom had threatened to shoot Dad. He said he didn't have any details, but she'd dialed 911 on Dad and when the police came, Dad was gone and Mom seemed confused. When Dad arrived home later, while the cops were still there, they took their stories and ultimately decided to take Mom to the psych ward at Swedish American Hospital, where she'd spend the next week or so. I couldn't reach David or Dad to see how she was doing; the only communication I'd receive would be from Bill.

This is when things started to get really weird and puzzling for me. Bill gave me daily updates on Mom as best he could, but the odd thing was that every time he went to see her, they would move her to another floor of the hospital and wouldn't tell him where she was. So Bill, clever as he is, simply sat down in the hospital and used his cell phone to call the main desk to find out what room she was in. They always told him on the phone this way, but whatever charade they were playing went on for the eight or nine days she was in the psych ward. When I've heard of other situations in which the police get involved without an arrest, they only put a forty-two hour hold on the person, but in Mom's case, they stretched it out to over a week.

On the eighth or ninth day Mom was in the hospital, Bill went in to see her as he did every day and was told that she had been transferred. When he asked where she was, they told Bill, one of her own sons, that he wasn't privy to that information. This confused me even more.

Bill was angry and confused at this point, so when he arrived back at his barber shop, he came up with a great idea. He had my nephew Goobs/Shane start to call all the nursing homes. The first four gave him the same answer when he called, that she wasn't there. On his fifth call, he contacted Alden Park Strathmoor Nursing Home. When he asked if Winifred Carol Wyman was there, their response was that they couldn't give out that information. Bingo, we then knew where she was.

After Bill called and told me how they had located Mom, I told him I made a few phone calls. My first call was to David. I asked him why Mom was in a nursing home dementia unit and his reply was, "She had her chance to go to assisted living, but now she's where she belongs." Then I asked him how long she would be there, and he said in a very cold voice, "Till the end." I was stunned, and Dave hung up on me before I could say goodbye. How heartless!

My next call was to my father. He said that yes, she was at Park Strathmoor when I asked. Then out of the blue, he asked me if I had any old girlfriends around, assuring me that he couldn't get it up anymore, but needed someone to clean, cook and talk to him. I was shocked that he had the balls to say that to me and I thought to myself how sick he was. I kept my thoughts to myself, but replied, "That's what you had a wife for." I didn't have any communication with Dad again until I went back to Rockford for a surprise visit.

The next day Bill and Goobs went out to Park Strathmoor to see Mom. They had no problem getting in, but what they found there shocked them. Mom was in a dementia ward with a roommate who was talking to her stuffed teddy bear. Mom, however, was acting like her normal self. Bill looked around the room and was sickened by what he saw.

When Mom asked Bill where she was, he replied, "You're in a prison with curtains."

During their forty-five minute visit, an older woman lay outside her door on the cold asphalt tiled floor in her own urine. This upset Goobs so much that he took a picture of her.

Bill and Goobs left the nursing home in tears. Bill couldn't believe that my father could be so cold as to compartmentalize his wife and keep her stored away like the rest of his things in life, as if she were a possession. How could he treat her like this after fifty-nine years of marriage?

On their drive back to the barber shop, Goobs texted me the picture of the woman on the floor. Meanwhile, Bill called Dad and ripped into him, demanding an explanation as to why he would treat his mother this way and further stated that he was going to terrorize him for what he did.

As soon as the nursing home found out about the picture, they banned Goobs from visiting, and Dad had Bill banned for threatening to terrorize him. He told the social worker for the nursing home that his wife was there for her safety, and Bill and Goobs were put on a no-call list.

When Bill relayed all this to me, I was stunned. I just couldn't believe this was happening. My brother Bill and his three sons had taken care of Mom and Dad for a very long time. Neither David nor Beth lived close enough to Rockford to help them. It was always Bill and his boys who would shovel snow, mow the yard and fix anything in the house for them. So this turn of events really had me buffaloed.

Bill and his children would still call or go to see Mom at Park Strathmoor. They either gave a fictitious name, or they would not sign in at all when they went to see Mom. Because this home was so poorly run, they got away with it.

I, on the other hand, was back at school. I'd spend hours on the computer, studying elder law and elder abuse. Little did I know when I started to do this, that it would consume the next year and a half of my life.

The first search I did on Google was elder abuse. The very first article I read discussed psychological abuse, and number one on that list was threatening to put an older person in a home against their will. This for me was a great place to start. My brother Dave and my father had already done this, and as far as I knew, it had gone on for many months.

As for physical abuse, Mother and we kids had suffered through my father's violent behavior from childhood into our teens. Even when we were young children, before my father's abuse was directed at us kids, he beat Mom in front of us on more than one occasion.

I also went to other sites on the computer that offered help in Illinois. There were many, including one called "Triad" which tried to put most of the programs under one umbrella. I studied all of these for hours on end, and with the help of Arthur, my roommate in Aspen, I printed as much material as possible. What I learned, however, I kept to myself. Since I was so far away from my family, I didn't want to upset the apple cart and be put on the no-call list and be isolated from Mom. By the way, isolation from family and friends is another form of elder abuse.

My studies went on for a few more weeks, but I had already decided to go to Rockford and assess the situation for myself. However, I wanted it to be a surprise visit, so I only told Bill in Rockford and Robin in San Diego and told them not to tell anyone else.

So, after twelve years of being with my girlfriend in San Diego on my birthday, I was headed to Rockford for my birthday and Mother's Day. Flying out of Aspen is always a trip for me. First of all, I hate flying, due to the fact that the sibling I lost was in an airplane crash. Secondly, I've done this every month for the past twelve and a half years to see Robin in San Diego. When I tell people this, they laugh and say it's probably why my relationship with her has lasted so long.

I had to get up at 3:00 a.m. to make my 7:00 a.m. flight. I caught the first leg to Denver which is about a twenty-five minute flight, with only a short layover before The flight on to Chicago. I settled into business class for my second leg only to be interrupted before take-off by a flight attendant who was dead-heading and started busting my chops for taking her seat. While sitting there, I could hear the flight attendants talking in the galley. When one of them said she was going to Rockford to see her parents in a nursing home, I immediately called out towards the galley, "Which high school?" The head of the perky blonde who'd given me a hard time about taking her seat peered around the corner and said, "Harlem," to which I replied, "Rockford West." We started up a conversation and I told her my name, and she told me her name and that she was travelling with her cat, or so I thought.

Her name was Kim J. I knew a Kim J. growing up but she looked a little younger than I. After the plane was in the air headed for Chicago, I started thinking about what was ahead for me in Rockford.

When we landed, I was pleasantly surprised to find out Kim and I had the same ground transportation, the bus. We sat together on the bus and talked for the whole hour and fifteen minute ride. We talked about our parents and the situations we were both in. I finally realized that she had a dog, not a cat, with her. I shrugged off that mistake by saying that it must've been the two Bloody Marys I had before take-off.

When we arrived in Rockford, we exchanged phone numbers and I told Kim I was busy, but asked her if she would call me later. I had no idea that she'd be one of my guardian angels on this journey. I didn't think of our connection as a love interest, but I'd never connected with a flight attendant in all my travels.

Bill picked me up at the Clock Tower Inn where the bus had let me off. I said goodbye to Kim with a hug you'd give your great-aunt. Then Bill and I drove directly to Park Strathmoor Nursing Home.

We talked along the way about what was going on with Mom, but I thought to myself "How bad can this be?" The home was on the more affluent east side. It had a major hospital with one hundred beds, and as we walked into the building, the first thing we saw was a grand piano. The staff was pleasant and it seemed very clean.

I walked up to the nursing station and told the gal behind the desk I was there to see Carol Wyman. She informed me there wasn't a Carol Wyman there. I looked over at Bill, feeling a little confused, and he said, "Winifred Carol Wyman." She replied, "Of course," and told us both to sign in. I went over, wrote down my scribble, and then Bill faked like he did.

The girl behind the desk then led us to a secured door. When we walked in, the hall was empty except for a couple of nurses and a few CNA's. Most of them were black. When I told a nurse we were there to see Winifred Carol Wyman, we were greeted by most of the staff hooting and laughing, saying, "Youse guys look like da Blues Brothers!" I suppose we did. My hair and Bill's were both in pony tails. I was dressed in a sport coat and Fedora, and we both had on dark sunglasses. We had a few laughs about that, then walked into the dining area where they were having lunch.

Most of the patients were sitting at tables for four, and I didn't see Mom at first. It didn't look so bad. Then I spotted Mom. She was helping the food servers serve juice and milk. When she saw me, her eyes lit up and she scurried over and gave me a hug and a big kiss on the cheek. We walked over to her table, pulled up two chairs, and Bill and I watched them eat lunch.

Everything seemed normal; that was until Mom introduced me to her table mates. There were two black men, one in a wheel chair and one with an old wooden cane. There was also a white woman about Mom's age.

The man with the cane would just sit, nod his head, and laugh but wouldn't say anything. The one in the wheel chair was crying and seemed upset while he ate. The woman just smiled and held her teddy bear. Meanwhile, Mom, Bill, and I were carrying on a fairly normal conversation, considering where she was and what she'd been through.

After lunch, we all went back to the room Mom shared with a roommate. The room was dark, even with the light on. There was a hospital curtain to separate their two old mechanical hospital beds with metal headboards made to look like fake wood. The walls were green-painted cinder block and there were curtains that covered windows that didn't open. Bill was right; Mom was in a prison with curtains. They also shared a Jack and Jill bathroom with the two men who were at our lunch table.

Mom sat propped up on her bed with me at the foot of the bed and Bill in the only guest chair in the room. Meanwhile, her roommate sat only a few feet from me on her bed, holding her teddy bear.

The door to Mom's room was open, and as I sat there, I realized that I was looking at the exact spot where the woman had lain on the floor in her own urine for forty-five minutes. That's when Goobs, my nephew, had taken the picture of her and had been barred from the nursing home.

As I started to speak to Mom, I noticed her suitcase and make-up kit were still packed and next to her bed, even though she'd been in the home for almost three weeks. I asked Mom if she was planning on going anywhere in a joking manner and she said, "Hell, yes. I think I'm going home with you, and furthermore, I'm tired of being in this snake pit,"

At that very moment I looked over to her roommate who was combing her stuffed teddy bear. She extended her stuffed toy and comb in my direction asked if I'd like to comb its hair for her. It was the first time I realized that Mom was R. P. McMurphy in <u>One Flew Over the Cuckoo's Nest</u>.

As Mom continued talking, she told me she wasn't allowed to use the phone, and if she didn't cooperate and take her medication at night, the nurses would hold her down and give her a shot in her hip to make her go to sleep. She also told me one of her kids, Bill, Marc, or Goobs, would sneak in a cell phone so she could call them. When the nurses would find them, they'd always hide her phone charger. Bill never told me but I'm sure he purchased quite a few trac phones. Mom went on to tell me that Dad would show up every few days and bring her Diet Coke and Hershey chocolate. Each time she'd ask him, "When am I going home?" and he'd just shake his head and say, "Soon."

On the other hand, I knew Bill would visit his mom every day, sometimes twice a day, and bring her Diet Coke and chocolate, and I thought to myself that she must have quite a stash.

After being in Mom's room for half an hour, Bill went to use the bathroom. While he was away, I was taken by surprise when my father walked into the room pushing one of the walkers with wheels, brakes, and a seat. He shuffled in and took a seat in the old chair Bill had vacated when he went to the bathroom.

I was cordial when I spoke to him, and asked him how he was doing, never letting on that I was upset at the situation he'd put his wife of fifty-nine years in. He replied that he was doing o.k. but needed a knee replacement and he had trouble walking very far because of congestive heart failure. Just then Bill came back into the room. He said "hi" to Dad, and even though he had put his mother away and had banned him from the nursing home, Bill found a way to be nice to him.

Unbeknownst to Dad, I was taping our whole conversation on my cell phone. We all chatted for a few minutes and then I asked Dad if we could take Mom out for my birthday and Mother's Day for brunch. Dad got a concerned look on his face and said, "No, Mom's not allowed to leave here." When I looked at him somewhat confused, I said, "Well, I'll go up to the front desk to see if they do a family meal at the nursing home for patients who can't leave." With that said, I got up and left the room and headed through the secured door to the front waiting area and desk.

There was no one at the desk when I arrived, so while I waited, I strolled over to take a look at the grand piano. The surface was rough, and when I pushed down on one of the ivories, I realized it didn't work. It was just a prop that made the place look warm and home-like, but only from a distance.

Just then the receptionist reappeared. I walked over and asked her if the nursing home did anything special for families on Mother's Day. She said, "No, we couldn't do that. We have over one hundred patients. If each family only brought four members, there'd be almost five hundred people and we aren't equipped for that." Before she could speak again,

I heard someone come up behind me. When I turned around, it was Dad. The receptionist then started talking again and said, "You can check your mom out for the day. Just have her back by eight at night."

Then I spoke up and said, "We'd only have her out from ten until two." I turned around and said to Dad, "Isn't that great?" I found it strange that he was already walking back to her room.

As he walked away I whispered to the girl behind the desk, asking, "Who has Carol's power of attorney?" and without saying a word, she pointed towards my father.

When I returned to the room, Bill and Dad were talking. I interrupted them, saying that I was tired because I'd been up since three that morning. But I talked long enough to make arrangements with Dad for brunch the next day at ten. He agreed. We said our goodbyes, hugged Mom, and then we left to go to Bill's house in the hood on the west side of Rockford. As we drove I felt better about Mom and thought that just maybe I could be a peace-maker for my family.

We drove through my old stomping grounds back to the family house in the hood. The visual triggered lots of memories for me, some good, some not. Things I hadn't thought about in years flashed through my mind.

As we pulled into the shared driveway, I looked up to the peak of the house, and in the small window I saw a skull. Right away, that brought back memories of the skull I'd found under the porch next door when I was nine.

We parked in back of the house. The first thing I noticed was a fence around a large deck on the back of the house, and the house next door where I'd found the skull was gone.

As I got out of the car, I heard the loud barking of three

huge dogs, a male and a female Rottweiler named Titan and Destiny, and a Dobie named Star. As Bill led me through the gate, he told me to take off my sunglasses and hat, that they wouldn't bite, and that they'd get used to me. I'd been bitten by dogs before in my life, but was never afraid of them. But here was three hundred pounds of pure muscle.

We made it into the kitchen where Bill gave me five slices of American cheese. It wasn't for me; it was to make a peace offering to the dogs. As they all sat down for the cheese, a little miniature pinscher, weighing about 15 pounds, appeared. It was my mom's dog that Bill had adopted sometime before Mom was put away. His name was Pierre, but I became accustomed to calling him Little Dog.

After I'd won the dogs over, Bill showed me into the living room where I would sleep since I was doing this trip on a very limited budget. My bed, which I would share with Little Dog, was an over-stuffed faux leather Lazy Boy.

We then toured the house, even the basement where there was a three feet by six feet area made up of odd patches of cement. I grabbed some food, ate, and then called Kim J., the flight attendant I'd met on the plane earlier and asked her if she'd like to meet for a drink. She agreed.

We met in Loves Park at a sports bar. She was dressed up and had make-up on and was taller and prettier than I remembered. We ordered up a couple of martinis, then talked for quite a while. How differently our families had handled the nursing home situation. Her family is in agreement and mine is so divided. It could have been the fact that both her parents were in the same home, even though her father was in better shape than her mother, who suffered from dementia. My parents, on the other hand, were estranged due to the fact that my father had put my mother somewhere she didn't want to be. The children, of course, would take sides.

After two drinks, we decided to go back to my brother's house and meet my family. The dogs love women, so we had no problem getting in the house. Bill, his two boys, Marc and Goobs, and their mother Kim were all having dinner, so we made another drink and lounged on the couches with the dogs while they ate.

After a bit, they finished eating. Goobs and his mother went off to the basement where they slept. Marc went out to celebrate his graduation from junior college with a double major in liberal arts and applied sciences, and Bill came into the living room to play blues guitar and talk with Kim J. and me about Mom's situation.

We sat and talked for about an hour or so when Bill headed up to his room. Seeing that we were pretty buzzed at the time, Kim and I fell asleep on our separate couches. At three in the morning, Kim woke up saying she had to go home, and we said goodbye. Then I climbed into my Lazy Boy chair which would be my bed for the next five days and went to sleep.

I awoke the next day with a bit of a hangover, something I'm not used to since I don't drink very much. I aroused the rest of the household, including the dogs, and got ready to take Mom, Dad and the family out for Mother's Day brunch and my birthday.

All of us, Bill, Marc and his fiancée Brooke, fourteen-year-old Matt, and I arrived at Park Strathmoor about fifteen minutes early, signed in, and went to Mom's room to wait for Dad. Mom was happy to see her kids, and they brought her cards and gifts for Mother's Day. It was great to see her having such a good time. We waited for Dad until about fifteen minutes past ten, because it's not unusual for my family to run late; in fact, it was always kind of a family joke.

I left the kids and Bill in Mom's room and walked up to the reception desk. I explained to the girl at the desk that we were there to take Carol Wyman to brunch. I told her we were waiting for my father, and wondered if we could check her out and have my father meet up with us at the restaurant.

She looked up and said, "Oh, Winifred Carol Wyman. Well, her husband called and said he wouldn't be here, and no one was allowed to take her out." At first I was shocked. Then I immediately called my dad's half-sister Pam and asked if she knew anything about this. She said Powell had told her that he wasn't going to brunch and that we couldn't take Mom anywhere. By that time I was getting more than a little pissed off, so I asked Aunt Pam where Dad was. She snapped back at me, "I'm not going to tell you." I was quiet for a moment and then told her I'd call later and that I loved her. She just said, "Goodbye," and hung up.

I was left with the lovely task of going back to Mom's room and telling everyone that Dad wasn't coming and Mom couldn't go. How nice. When I shared this news, there were more than a few tears. My blood was boiling at this point, but I decided to bury it and go out to brunch and make the best of a really bad situation. As we left, I told Mom that I'd figure something out and would see her the next day.

We made the best of brunch, with me hacking on my nephews, since I hadn't spent time with them in years. I gave Marc grief about being a twitch because he'd worry about what makes Jell-O wiggle; I didn't hack much on nephew Goobs because he's kind of like a little girl.

After brunch, we went back to Bill's. I slipped out back to sneak a little puff off a joint just to calm my nerves. Everyone else was in the empty lot playing bocce ball, so I joined in. We talked about what to do for Mom next and discussed the power of attorney, so Brooke went inside to

Google it on the computer.

While Brooke was in the house, we continued to play bocce ball on the same lot where I had found the skull. I was explaining it and making jokes about it to Marc and Matt. Bill and I had never brought the skull up to each other, much less to his children. We hadn't talked about it at all in all these years.

Brooke came out about the time we were done with bocce ball and had me come in to look at what she'd discovered. I started reading the website with all the Illinois laws for a POA and was pleased to find out that Mom, since she hadn't been adjudicated, could sign a new one and it would be good as gold. It would give me the power to make any health decisions, including her placement in the nursing home, and I could take her wherever I wanted. She still had rights!

To make a power of attorney legal, all Mom had to do was sign it and have two people of legal age who aren't family witness it. So we made a plan to go get Mom out.

Marc was the only one who didn't agree with the plan. He thought he could just call his grandpa and straighten this out. He got my dad on the phone and asked what was going on. His grandpa's only reply was, "Don't mess with me, Boy. I'll get ya." This must have crushed Marc because he was grandpa's closet grandson. Marc was now on board with us.

I then called Kim J. to see if she'd like to come to dinner and have her hair done, which I'd promised earlier. She said "yes" and came on over. As we ate dinner, I explained to Kim what had transpired that day. She was just beside herself and couldn't believe it.

During the course of the evening, I think I had two

drinks, but I could see Kim getting pretty buzzed. I decided it was time to get her hair done while she was still with us. I finished her hair; then Goobs decided to put make-up on her. She was still drinking and feeling pretty good when Goobs asked if she had her nipple pierced, and when she said, "No," he offered to do it for her. After a little more coaxing, she said, "I'll do it if John does." I thought about it for a millisecond and decided, nah, I wouldn't know how to explain my pierced nipple to Robin, and I didn't want to see Kim's boobs that bad. When Goobs was done with her make-up, she looked pretty damn hot and with her new do and all; what could you say?

Goobs left to go to the gay bar for some event, and Kim J., Bill, and I watched a movie in the living room. At some point, Bill went to bed, and I fell asleep in my chair, and Kim J. was out cold on the couch.

I was woken up by the dogs barking and woke Kim up so she could drive home. She wasn't sure how to get back, so I jumped into Bill's Blazer and she followed me to her destination. I honked and waved goodbye from the car.

When I got back home, Bill had coffee on and Brooke handed me the power of attorney forms. I took a shower and waited for my other witness for the POA We had already decided that the boys' mom, Kim B., would be one since she and Bill were never married. The other one would be Tiffany, one of Goobs' "fruit flies," girls who hang out with gay guys.

I was nervously pacing the floor when Tiffany arrived, apologizing for being late and saying she'd meet us at the nursing home. Kim and I took off in the car and caught up with small talk about her life, the kids, and, of course, Mom.

When we arrived at the nursing home, Tiffany was already there and my nervousness left. The three of us walked into Park Strathmoor, signed in, and went to Mom's room. She was happy to see us. I explained the power of attorney to her, and let her read over it before she signed it.

Just then, I heard a shuffle by the door and asked one of the girls to close it. Mom proceeded to sign the POA, knowing she'd be going with me. Kim and Tiffany both signed the witness section and then I grabbed Mom's bags and opened the door to the hall. I was surprised to find three of the black nurses on duty blocking my exit. I explained to them that Mom had just signed a new POA naming me as her agent. The head nurse took the document and started reading it very slowly. I grabbed it out of her hand, stating that she knew what it was and showed her the signatures.

With the POA in hand, I asked the nurse to step aside since I knew what the document meant and she couldn't hold me any longer. Since we were U.S. citizens, she couldn't hold us against our will. That would be kidnapping.

She stepped aside and yelled to another nurse to call 911. As we walked to the secured door, a CNA and an orderly both said, "John, ya doin' da right thing. Yo mamma don't belong in there." I asked them if they would testify, to which they responded, "No sir, we'd lose our jobs."

When we got to the door, Kim had forgotten the code to get out, and I never knew it. By then the nurses had gathered at the other end of the hall and were laughing at us. I kept telling them to please open the door, that they were holding us against our will. They might as well have been deaf.

Kim finally got Bill on his cell phone and he told her the code. She punched it in and we were on our way. The girls took off together while I walked Mom to Bill's car. She was happy, but kind of squinting since she hadn't been in the sun for over a month.

Just as I was about to back out, two white vans pulled in behind me, blocking me in. Then four police officers emerged, two from each van. I got out of the car, leaving Mom inside, and walked up to the first officer. I introduced myself and handed him the power of attorney document and explained what I was doing and what had just happened.

He didn't understand the POA, so he called his shift supervisor. By the time he arrived, another squad car had shown up and so had my father. Apparently, the nursing home had called him too. I now had seven men with seven guns to deal with. You'd have thought I'd robbed a bank or shot someone.

I was in the car calming Mom down because she had started to cry. I assured her everything would be o.k. Then there was a tap on my window. I got out of the car, not the least bit nervous, and introduced myself to the shift supervisor, Ken F. I stood by the door to Bill's car and explained to Ken what had just happened, handing him the power of attorney.

Meanwhile, while he read the document, another officer started to question Mom. I intervened and asked him to handle her with kid gloves since she was upset. During all this I could feel my father glaring at me while he sat pathetically in his walker across the parking lot surrounded by the same nurses who had held me against my will.

After Ken had read the document, he walked over to my father and the nurses for a conference. I stayed outside the car, talking to another fairly young officer who was quite sympathetic and said, "I understand. We all have mothers too."

When the supervisor Ken F. came back to talk with me, he said, "I don't quite understand this POA, but if you get it notarized by an attorney, you can come back with an officer tomorrow, and you can take her then."

If I had known then what I know now, I would have just driven away. That POA was as good as gold and didn't have to be notarized. It was protected under federal law. There were, however, seven of them and only one of me. You could say I was out-gunned!

I reluctantly agreed as long as I could walk Mom back to her room. They agreed, so I grabbed Mom's bags and explained that I'd be back the next day for her and started to walk toward the building. Mom had tears in her eyes. As I looked over toward the nurses and my father, to the surprise of the police, I held the POA up in my hand while I shouted across the parking lot that they were not to drug her. I told them that I was her agent now. I would find out much later that they did drug her that day!

When I finally got Mom back to her room, she had stopped crying. I gave her a hug and told her I loved her, something I hadn't said to her in years. I then settled her back in her room and told her I'd see her the next day.

As I walked to my car, I stopped and thanked the officers. I told them I'd call them the next day as soon as I got the power of attorney notarized.

I drove away and immediately called Kim B., who had just been with me and asked her if she knew a lawyer who could notarize the document. She said she'd make a few calls and call me back. As I drove toward the West Side, Kim called and told me to meet her by the courthouse downtown. We met up and walked up to Attorney J.F. Heckinger's office. I personally can't stand lawyers, but I needed one, so on into his office we went. He introduced himself; then we all took our seats. I explained what had just taken place at Park Strathmoor and that

I just needed the power of attorney notarized. He did so and didn't charge me, saying that he owed Kim a favor. We left his office with a notarized document, but there was something about him. He looked as crooked as a dog's hind leg.

I got back to Bill's house later that afternoon and called Kim J. to see if she wanted to go to dinner that evening, telling her I'd explain what had taken place that day. I also called Robin in San Diego and told her about my day, and she couldn't believe it.

Kim J. met me at Bill's house and then I drove us to dinner at Maria's, my favorite Italian restaurant. I knew the owner Johnny C., so after we were seated I went to the kitchen to hack on him a little. He gave me a big hug, then walked me out to my table to meet Kim. He bought us a drink and styled us out with food. I told Kim what happened at the nursing home and asked her how her parents were doing. She replied that her mother wasn't doing very well mentally and her father wasn't doing well physically. I told her I felt sorry for her, but she assured me they were getting the best care they could.

After dessert, Kim told me that if I got my mom out the next day, she'd like to help me drive back to Denver with her. I said that would be an enormous help and that I'd take her up on her offer. After paying the bill, I drove Kim J. back to her car, gave her a hug and a kiss on the cheek and we said our goodbyes. Little did I know I'd never see her again.

By the time I got home, I was exhausted after all that adrenalin rushed through my veins. I immediately fell asleep as I climbed into my Lazy Boy with Little Dog.

As soon as I dozed off, Bill screamed from upstairs to hit the floor. The dogs were barking and there were distinct gun shots outside the door. After I lay on the floor for about five minutes, Bill came down and gave me an "all clear." He said that when I heard gunfire, the floor was the safest place to be because only the front door and the living room window were bullet-proof. While that wasn't really reassuring, I climbed back in my chair and fell fast asleep.

The next morning came too quickly. I got up at seven with Bill, had coffee, and then got ready. I took off for the nursing home with Kim B. after we called an officer to meet us. We were told not to go on the property until he got there.

We waited outside for about fifteen minutes, talking about what I'd do when I took Carol back to Aspen. Before I could gather many thoughts on that, the officer arrived. He got out of his car and walked over to us. I handed him the notarized POA, and after he looked over the document, he said he had some bad news. He told me my father had filed for emergency guardianship, and it was in the court pipeline. I wouldn't be allowed to take Mom that day.

Kim B. and I got in the car and left. Now I'm no dummy, so I knew a case in the pipeline wasn't valid until it was signed by a judge. My power of attorney was still in effect, so I dropped Kim B. off at home and went straight to Bill's barber shop.

I took a toke off a puffy before I went into Bill's shop, just to calm myself down. I felt like someone had just kicked me in the balls. I couldn't have been any angrier, or so I thought.

I took up a chair in Bill's waiting area until he finished his customer. Then I told Bill what went down. His only reply was, "That's how the system works here in Rockford." I'm not exactly sure how I responded, but it was probably something about corruption, or bullshit, or whatever.

Then I asked Bill if he could take the rest of the day off, since both his sons were working. Until I was notified, I still had power of attorney and I wanted to make a few stops to obtain some medical information.

Bill saw no problem, so off we went. As we drove, I told Bill we were going to Rockford Memorial and Swedish American hospitals for records. I also wanted to talk to Bruce Person, a licensed clinical social worker. I forgot to tell Bill, but when I was working with Dave on what to do about Mom, he made a crucial mistake and gave me Bruce's name. David and Dad had taken Mom to Bruce for an evaluation on March 3, 2009. When I called Bruce at that time, he told me he'd given Mom the mini dementia test and that she had passed it with 28 out of 30 questions correct. His conclusion was that she didn't have dementia, and his diagnosis was very, very important.

Our first stop was Swedish American Hospital. I went in and they directed me to another building for records. We went up the elevator to the top floor and walked up to the desk. Bill and I talked to the ladies, and I showed them my document and driver's license. They were very nice and said it would take a few minutes and that we should have a seat.

Ten minutes went by and then they reappeared with a small stack of papers. They had me sign some sort of release. Bill and I both thanked them, and I snatched up the papers and asked them how much I owed them. They said there was no charge. I didn't know it at the time, but while I was talking to one gal, Bill was telling the other one the whole story. He even went as far as showing her the picture Goobs had taken of the lady on the floor of the nursing home in her own urine. I think this information softened them up a bit.

When we got in the car, I immediately started reading the report. As I read, I became more than shocked; I was sickened. The report wasn't complete, but it gave me a full picture of what happened on April third when Mom called 911 on Dad.

The report from the hospital stated that Winifred Carol Wyman had been brought in on a forty-eight hour psychiatric hold because she'd been drinking and had threatened to kill her husband for fooling around with the cleaning lady. It was strange that she could still be jealous after fifty-nine years of marriage. For as long as I could remember, that had been my father's modus operandi.

The picture was starting to become clearer. There definitely was a pattern of isolating Mom from the kids she loved so much. This was evident when she had been moved around the hospital to hide her from Bill.

My father's own words in the report were that he thought Mom was delusional, especially when she drank, and to calm her down he was giving her his own sleeping pills, Ambien. Giving someone else your prescription drugs is, of course, illegal, and the combination of the drugs and alcohol could be devastating.

Further in the report, Powell admitted that the cleaning lady was with him in his bedroom with the door closed. But he said Mom should've known he wasn't cheating on her, because she knew he had been impotent since his prostate surgery which he had in his mid-sixties.

Dad had started to weave his web of deceit. I just wondered when he'd get tangled up in it. He went on to state that Carol suffered from dementia and he had taken her to a psychiatrist who had prescribed Aricept. Dad said he hadn't bought it because he couldn't afford it. That's when I realized that David and Powell had been doctor shopping Mom. I had also read that under Illinois law, denying someone needed medication falls under elder abuse.

Sometime in late April, Powell had told his grandson Marc that he'd just purchased a laptop computer. I found this odd since he couldn't afford Mom's prescription. Not that I thought she even needed it, but these situations looked like more criminal elder abuse. But the agencies involved at the time just weren't getting it.

We pulled up to Bruce's office, but before going in, I read the final diagnosis from Swedish American, which just floored me. It stated that Mom had the following: dementia, Alzheimer's, homicidal and suicidal tendencies, alcoholism, and schizophrenia. If this were the case, then why wasn't Mom in a mental institution? If she were homicidal, why did she have a roommate in the nursing home? It just didn't make any sense.

I'd called Bruce somewhere along the way, so he was expecting us. He came out and greeted us and ushered Bill and me back to his office. He stated he wouldn't have much time because he was in between patients. We both took a seat, and, as usual, I did most of the talking for Bill and me. I told Bruce that I'd just read the psychiatric report on the way to his office and couldn't quite believe it, especially since we had a conversation in early March on the phone after Dave had given me the wrong office to call.

I then handed the report over to Bruce. As he read it, a questioning look came over his face. After he finished, I told him Mom had always had some problems; she'd take things that didn't belong to her, but were insignificant to someone else. Then she'd lie about it. She would also often exaggerate stories that weren't completely true to start with. But she'd been this way for as long as I could remember. Maybe, just maybe, she'd always been sick, just not as sick as my father.

Bruce handed the report back to me and at the same time gave me his records since I still held power of attorney. He told me again that David had called and said his mother was sundowning (showing confusion at the end of the day) and had dementia. Powell would then make an appointment for Carol, based on David's assumptions. Bruce then stated that after testing Carol, he'd found no signs of dementia. He also found it peculiar that Powell, when asked to, refused to sit in on the interview with Mom.

Bill, who had offered only a few words during this whole encounter, handed Bruce the picture of the lady on the floor at Park Strathmoor. This drew Bruce's ire, and before he went back to his next patient, I told him I had one more question. If my mother had passed all those tests on March third, was it possible she had some sort of accelerated dementia? Bruce instantly said, "No, dementia's a slow moving disease. It just doesn't happen like that." Bill and I both thanked Bruce for his time. I let him know what was happening with Mom and asked him to keep in touch.

As Bill and I drove back to his shop, not a word was spoken. We'd just exchange glances with puzzled looks on our faces. I dropped Bill off and told him I'd meet him at the house later that evening.

Back at the house I took another shower and smoked a joint afterwards, just to relax. I called Kim J., the flight attendant, and brought her up to speed on what I'd done that day. She again offered to help me drive Mom to Denver and with that said, I told her I'd call her the next day.

I went back to the shop to pick up Bill, but he was still working on a customer. He told me to go over the old North Main Tap and meet Bobby Jr. It had been one of my old haunts from my youth, and I'd just found out the old man had passed. I thought I'd better go over and introduce myself and give my condolences to his son.

Bobby was a spitting image of his father. We talked for awhile and exchanged stories about how wild his father was. Then Bill came to the bar to get me. The North Main Tap would become my new haunt, my "Cheers" for the next year and a half.

Bill and I went home and joined Marc and nephew Goobs for dinner. As we ate we filled the boys in on what went on that day, gathering information on Grandma. I'd be on the computer most of that night, looking up the different elder abuse laws and what Mom's rights were.

When everybody was long asleep in their beds, I turned on the computer and went to work. It didn't go so smoothly at first, because I was used to working on an Apple. But once I found my way around the P.C., I rolled. For anyone doing research, the use of a computer is paramount. Most of the information on elder law and abuse is accurate, and the hotline and crisis lines are endless. After an hour or so, my eyes grew weary and my point of focus was diminishing. By then I think I had enough information and notes for the time being, so I shut the P.C. down.

It was about 2:00 a.m. and I sat at the dining room table. I started a journal to record the events in order, beginning in January with David's call about Mom. Suddenly, I heard loud music outside, which doesn't happen often in Aspen. When I went to investigate the source of the music, I was surprised to see about fifteen neighbors dancing in the street. This was in front of the house where the gunfire had erupted a few days before.

I don't know what I was thinking, but I just headed out the front door, only to find myself in the middle of a bunch of drug-dealing, gun-toting gangbangers. For some reason, this sorry white ass middle-aged man didn't feel any fear. As they all looked at me, I just said, "I was born and raised in this hood, and just want to get some video of ya'll dancing in the streets so I can show everyone where I'm from and how it rolls in da hood." I stayed out there with them for only about fifteen minutes. They didn't say much and I didn't want to wear out my welcome, so after I videotaped them doing the splits and going upside down on the asphalt, and watching a couple of drug deals go down, I decided it was time to try to get some sleep!

I tossed and turned as much as you can in a Lazy Boy chair with Lil' Dog on top of me. I must've dozed off when suddenly this loud knocking on the front door woke me up. I looked up and it was 6:00 a.m. In the four days I'd been at Bill's, no one had ever even used the front door.

As I lumbered out of my chair and went to the front door, I could hear the others who were sleeping start to stir. The four dogs were doing what they were supposed to, making a lot of noise.

When I opened the door, I was greeted by a not so friendly looking sheriff's deputy with a stack of papers the size of a big city phone book. He asked for my name in an authoritative voice. When I replied, "John," he said, "John Wyman?" I nodded and he handed me a part of the stack of papers, then asked if any of the rest of the family were home. I nodded affirmatively. About that time I heard Bill coming downstairs, which was behind me. Then the officer said in a commanding military style voice to get them all up and into the living room.

Once we'd all gathered, he handed papers to the rest of us. He proceeded to explain in an unfriendly voice that the papers were orders of protection filed by my father, their grandfather, against us. He explained that we were to have zero contact with my father, even through a third party, and were not to go on the property at the nursing home to see their grandmother. To do so would result in a felony arrest. You don't argue with the cops in the hood, because they're the only ones with guns who are authorized to use them, and they will.

After the officer left, I looked around the room, noticing the color had left my nephew Marc's face. I asked him what was wrong. He told me that the order of protection would wreck his career in health care, and that he wouldn't be able to go to school. I instantly thought to myself, how could my father, so close to the end of his life, do such a thing to his grandson, who was just starting his. Then again, this was the same son-of-a-bitch who threw his wife away after fifty-nine years of marriage. Marc was truly hurt.

By this time, Bill had collapsed on the floor behind me, sobbing and crying so hard he could hardly breathe. As his sons huddled around him on the floor as if they were in a rugby scrum, I could only make out every other word Bill said. Through his sobbing, I finally understood that here was a fifty-two-year-old man realizing he may never see his mom again, and he was the one who had taken care of her since I'd left for Aspen twenty-eight years before.

After everyone had calmed down, I knew I'd need legal counsel, so I called J.F. and he said to come to his office immediately. When I arrived at his office, I was able to see him right away and handed him the order. He cocked one eyebrow and then told me my father had also filed for emergency guardianship. He knew who Dad's attorney was and even stated that Sharon Rudy was one of his best friends and we could probably work something out. I was uneasy with him, but had very little time and very little choice. He asked for a retainer, so I gave him two hundred dollars in cash and with that he said he'd see me in court on June 16, 2010. I said goodbye, but still had this unsettling feeling in my stomach, like I'd been had.

I went back to Bill's and called my Aunt Pam to see what was going on. I first asked her how she felt and how her health was. She was curt when she responded, and her only words, and the last I would hear from her, were, "You're not going to win this one."

I didn't quite know what to make of her statement. My only response was, "I love you," and said goodbye.

My next call was to Kim J. I told her what had happened and thanked her for waiting around to help me drive Mom back to safety in Colorado. Then I added, "That ain't happening."

She said that since we weren't leaving, she'd go visit Mom with her Little Dog and would call me to give me a report on her condition before she flew back to Denver the next morning.

I, too, was to fly out the next day, but I still had a few more loose ends to tie up. My first stop was to obtain more records, so I went to Rockford Memorial Hospital. They were very efficient, but they only found a record from 1996 when my brother Dave had called and said his mother smelled of alcohol on the PHONE. I found that odd since that phone technology hasn't been invented yet. After David brought her in for an evaluation, the doctor found no signs of alcoholism. I wondered then how long they'd been doing this to Mom, and why.

Meanwhile, Brooke, Marc's fiancée, had gone on the computer only to find that Powell had lied extensively on the orders, which turned out to be a class four felony. Since Marc hadn't been any part of what I'd been up to since my arrival in Rockford, he shouldn't have been on the order at all. He was just crushed. He was so upset that he called David's wife Krista to see what was happening. She informed Marc that she had filed an order of protection against David when he'd beat her in December of 2008. When Marc asked about the alcohol at Mom and Dad's house, she stated that they quit bringing in hard liquor and only brought wine to her. As Marc told me about his conversation with Krista, it only raised more questions in my mind. If they thought Carol had a problem and wasn't allowed out of the house, why would they enable her by giving her any alcohol at all?

When David found out Krista had talked with Marc, he went after her again, and she had the order reinstated. It then occurred to me how very little I knew about that part of my family.

My next call was to the DA's office to let them know my father had perjured himself on the orders of protection, but they just didn't seem to care.

Since this had taken up most of my day, my last call was to Kim J. who had gone to see Mom that day. When I finally reached her, I asked if we could get together, but she told me she was too busy since she was leaving the next morning. Then she went on to tell me about her visit with Mom.

Now Mom didn't know Kim, but she was glad to have company, especially her Little Dog. Kim went on to tell me how pleasant and talkative Mom was, and that she'd spent an hour and a half with her. I was pleased to hear this and told her I'd catch up with her back in Aspen. I invited her to come up to the High Country and I'd introduce her to some of my wealthy male friends. I thanked her for all her help, and we said our goodbyes, not knowing we'd never see each other again. It's strange how people come and go in your life, and even in a short time can have such a great effect.

I went to bed early that night, but it wasn't a restful sleep. Bill got up early and drove me to the airport. We rehashed everything that had happened that week in disbelief. When he dropped me off, he told me, "Love ya' bro," and I said the same in response. I'd see him in mid-June for the protection order hearing.

As I slumped into my seat on the plane, my mind was racing, thinking of Dad, but all that would come out was, "How dare he? Why would he? How could he?" As the plane took off, I felt like I was escaping. Little did I know what a long journey lay ahead of me and how absurd this whole ordeal with Mom would become.

CHAPTER IX

LET THE ABSURD BEGIN

Home at last, home at last. Arthur, my roommate, picked me up at the airport, and I didn't waste any time before telling him what went down in Rockford. As we drove to my metal cabin on the river, I filled him in on my angel flight attendant, my brother's house in the hood, and what I'd just been through. As I talked, I suddenly realized how very little my friend knew about the life I had left behind. I had known Art for almost thirty years, and I had never talked about my life before Aspen.

Art listened intently as we drove. I'm sure I was talking as fast as a machine gun, but Art's source of income was transcribing minutes from congressional meetings on the computer, a job that hadn't yet been outsourced to another country, so he was able to digest everything I told him as fast as I could talk.

We soon arrived at my metal cabin on the river. I call it that because in all actuality it's a trailer on the river in a mobile home park that I co-own with my girlfriend Robin. But for her to admit that verbally would be like vinegar coming back out her mouth.

When I went into the trailer, I set my luggage in the living room, went straight back to my hair salon, which is attached to the trailer, sat down at the desk, and turned on my computer. I took out my protection order and started to study it only to realize that my father had filed an emergency guardianship. As I started to Google the meaning and laws that applied to the order of protection and the guardianship, things started to appear much clearer.

I discovered that granting a person guardianship of another is one of the most radical things you can do. It basically strips a person of the rights granted to United States citizens. It deprives a person of the right to self-determination regarding financial or health care decisions. It allows the courts and the guardian to have full and absolute control over another's life. The knowledge of what my father had done to his wife and his kids recently and in the past combined with Bruce Person's diagnosis of my mother created a situation that tore into the depths of my soul. As for the order of protection, I realized I could be arrested in any of the fifty states. Even making a civil telephone call to a third party could result in a felony arrest warrant.

But I don't quit easily, so I simply delved into my computer to learn every aspect of my mother's rights, my rights, and just about every law or article on elder abuse. This is a scene that I would recreate almost every night for the next twelve months, to the point that it would most certainly affect my physical being, as well as my mental health.

During the ensuing weeks before I was to return to Rockford for the hearing on the order of protection, I made many phone calls to the various government agencies that were supposed to help someone like my mother in this situation. First, I tried to obtain legal counsel for Mom through Prairie State Legal Services, which is a non-profit organization that helps people who can't afford an attorney. I was told that my mother would have to contact them herself. I tried to explain that this would be impossible since my father had isolated her and she was forbidden to use a phone. They just didn't seem to care.

Then, while reading the guardianship paper, I found out my mom was appointed a guardian ad litem, whose job, as I understood it, was to be the ears and eyes of the court. Her name was Ruth R. I tried numerous times to contact her and finally received a response. I described to her my father's emotional and physical abusiveness, his denial of prescribed medication and administration of his sleeping pills to Mom, and his isolation of her to the point she couldn't even obtain legal counsel. I also repeated Bruce Person's report that she displayed no signs of dementia, or anything else for that matter. I even pointed out that my father had lied on the order of protection.

After Ruth listened to my list of allegations, she said she'd take my information into consideration. From her tone of voice, however, I felt she was just walking through the steps of being a guardian ad litem because it was easy money, but I really didn't know for sure.

As I prepared for my journey back to Rockford for the protection hearing, I had to ask myself if trying to save Mom from being in a place where she didn't belong was worth pursuing. If it hadn't been for my brother Bill and his children being so upset, or my mother's two sisters, Phyllis and Marilyn, I'd probably have given up and gone back to my routine of flying out to San Diego or Chicago every three weeks to be with my girlfriend. But that was not to be.

My only other call before I embarked on my journey back to Rockford for the hearing was to my lawyer J.F. to explain to him my father's felonious behavior and to have him contact Bruce Person for his evaluation of my mother. His only response was that he'd see me in court on the sixteenth of June.

The night before I left for Rockford I decided I'd need to cut off my long curly hair that had taken years to grow and was my trademark look. I took my clippers and gave myself a haircut for the first time in my career. It didn't look so good when I was done, but I knew my brother Bill or one of his kids could fix it before court since they were all barbers.

By the time I finished packing, which didn't take very long because my luggage hadn't budged from the living room since my last trip, it was three a.m. I dozed for a couple of hours before catching the seven a.m. flight to Chicago.

While on the plane to O'Hare, I pondered the situation I was going home to in Rockford. I thought about the fact that I hadn't seen Robin in two months. I reflected on the disdain I felt for the judicial system, knowing that justice and law have little to do with each other. Add to these my distrust of lawyers in general, and it made for a restless flight.

After I arrived at O'Hare, I caught the bus to Rockford where Bill picked me up and then drove directly to his shop to give me a proper businesslike haircut. I then took his Jeep, dropped my luggage off at his house in the hood, and drove another hour and a half to the south side of Chicago to Robin's father's house to pick up my only suit, an Armani knock-off, which still stood the test of time.

Since I was already down there, I went out to my favorite pizza place, Aurelio's, with my faux nephews Andy, Ben, and Sam, their parents David and Jennifer, and Robin's father, Jerry. I told them as best I could what was going on, without dominating the whole conversation, because I wanted it to be a pleasant meal, and I think by this time they knew how fucked up my family was. After dinner they all wished me good luck, and, boy, did I need luck. Then as quickly as I had arrived, I was driving back to Bill's house in the hood.

I got there at one a.m. and was pretty damn tired. I was greeted by Bill's alarm system, two Rottweiler's, one

Dobie, and Lil' Dog, the mini-Pinscher. I went into the house and everyone was sleeping, so I curled up in the Lazy Boy with Lil' Dog for the rest of what was left of the night.

I awoke before everyone else, showered, shaved and put on my suit. Then I nervously paced the living room as the rest of the house woke up and got ready for court. I was so upset that I even lost my appetite and didn't eat anything before court, and that was very unlike me.

We all arrived downtown at the courthouse. I hadn't been downtown in thirty years and never in the courthouse. My only experience there was shining shoes outside for the lawyers and judges when I was eleven or twelve years old.

As we all gathered outside the courtroom, I was somewhat anxious since my attorney hadn't arrived. Here we were, six family members filling the corridors. My brother Bill and his four kids had their own attorney, who'd already arrived, and I was still waiting nervously for mine.

I thought my dad would have to be there, but he was nowhere around. After forty-five minutes or so, J.F., my lawyer, showed up waltzing in with this small round lady in comfortable shoes who I later realized was my father's attorney, Sharon Rudy.

As our group was ushered into the courtroom, my lawyer took me aside to a small conference room and told me that he, my brother's lawyer, and Shari R. were going into the judge's chamber for a conference with the judge and that I should wait.

After fifteen minutes or so, J.F. reappeared in the small conference room and explained the great deal he'd made. He told me if I wouldn't present all my evidence at this hearing they'd drop the order of protection against all of us. This would mean that my nephew Marc and his girlfriend Brooke could enter their chosen professions, which were to start the following week, and I'd be able to present my case at Mom's adjudication hearing on July 9th. However, if we tried to contact my father even through a third party, the orders would be reinstated. For me, this didn't sound like such a great deal. It would mean traveling back again in three weeks for Mom's hearing. I agreed, though, for my nephew's sake and fell on my sword for his career.

I then entered the courtroom to hear the judge's ruling. He set the order aside, explained to all six of us defendants that they would be reinstated if they were violated, and made one more comment that still haunts me to this day. He said the orders of protection my father had brought forth were without merit!

With that I walked out of the courtroom, looked over at my lawyer with slight frustration and disgust, and said, "I'll see you July 9th."

On the way back to Bill's barbershop we stopped for cigs at a gas station. There I ran into two old friends I'd known from my youth, Joe and George. They were surprised to see me in Rockford and especially in a suit. I told them why I was back in Rockford and what my father had done and asked if they had any connections in town that could still get things done, if you know what I mean.

George responded and said to stop by the station later and talk to his brother Clicquo. I really didn't want to ask for a favor, but felt like I was running out of options.

Later that night, after I'd dumped the suit and threw on jeans and a tee shirt, I met up with Clicquo at the North Main Tap. We went outside to talk while I had a smoke. I gave him an abbreviated version of what was happening. He told me he knew a judge and would call her. I thought that meant later, since it was 8:00 p.m., but no, he just took out his cell phone and called her right there. He asked me if I wanted to see her right then. I replied that I didn't think we should bother her that late, so I arranged to meet her at the courthouse at 8:00 a.m. the next day. Now, I thought to myself, I might still be able to get things done in Rockford through the backdoor, just like old times.

I gathered myself together the next morning and put on some nice threads. I dropped Bill off at the shop and headed downtown to the courthouse. As I drove, the turf became all too familiar to me, triggering memories of days gone by, the luxury high rise I lived in during my twenties, and the preschool we'd walk to to pick up my baby brother when Bill and I were in junior high. Then I drove by the Beattie Park on the river where I gave Jill Neff her first kiss. These were pleasant memories that diverted my attention from my journey.

When I arrived at the courthouse, I grabbed my small folder and headed through security and on to the corridors outside the courtrooms to wait for the judge. After waiting for about ten minutes, I went back downstairs to the clerk's office to find out where I could find her. They sent me back upstairs to her office where I explained to the receptionist why I was there.

She had me take a seat and said, "I'll let you know when the judge gets here. However, you're not on her daily calendar." After waiting for about thirty minutes, I got a little anxious, so I told her secretary that I was going back down to the courtroom. Not finding her there, I headed back up to her office. As I entered, I was greeted by a not so friendly bailiff who asked me who I wanted to see and who sent me there. As he came toward me, I backed out of the office, answering his questions with one word, "Clicquo." He asked for his last name, so I simply turned around and walked away. I never did get to see a judge that day, but I didn't give up my source.

Disappointed and somewhat frustrated, I headed back to the car. Along the way I thought, "I tried; at least I tried." I got in the car and headed over to Catholic Charities where Terri, my mom's appointed ombudsman, worked. The duties of the court appointed guardian ad litem and the ombudsman kind of blurred into one another, but they were both supposed to be advocates for Mom.

After I checked in at the desk, I took a seat, looked around, and realized that the place was bustling with people there for aid, or whatever services they offered. After twenty minutes or so, the receptionist came over and led me to Terri's office. After short introductions, I settled in to talk, giving her all the information I had from Bruce Person and the hospitals and explained my father's behavior and the isolation of my mother. Terri responded by saying she'd look it over. However, she felt my mother was where she needed to be, saying she was delusional and kept repeating she was in the "snake-pit." I again reiterated she should look over the documents and that I'd call her when I returned to Aspen.

Leaving Terri's office, I not only felt like an out-of-towner, I also felt like a foreigner in a familiar, but oh so different, place. It was not the place I remembered growing up in. It was like Jimmy Stewart returning to Bedford in It's a Wonderful Life.

As I drove back up State Street, a sudden rush of days gone by raced through my mind. Glimpses of my first apartment and the first salon I worked at when I was only eighteen flooded me with memories of being young and carefree. Back then, I had no worries at all, unlike the complicated situation I found myself in.

When I arrived at the Visiting Nurse Association office, I walked in, talked to the receptionist, and handed her my power of attorney, which as far as I knew, was still in effect. She took my information and led me back to the director's office.

The director came in, introduced herself, and offered me a chair. As we sat and talked, I asked most of the questions. She assured me my mother had been removed from her home for her own safety. She said the house was uninhabitable and filthy with goat paths going everywhere.

In response, I asked why, if it was unsafe for my mother, was it okay for my father, who has always been a hoarder, to live there. Furthermore, why wasn't the information I'd given them on my father's behavior ever considered in this case. The director had no explanation. I pleasantly thanked her for her time and left, still feeling frustrated. As I drove away, I realized I forgot to ask her for a report, but figured I could always ask for it later.

I then drove to Bill's house, got out of my suit, and relaxed for awhile. About four o'clock that afternoon, after I'd repacked my luggage for the return trip to Aspen, I headed to Bill's shop and the North Main Tap.

When I walked into Bill's salon, he was still busy clipping someone's hair, so I slipped over to the Tap. They were becoming familiar with my face again, so after ordering up a Grey Goose Martini, I asked if I could play their slot machines. Even though the machines had signs on them proclaiming they were for entertainment only. In reality, if you're a local, they pay off just like Vegas. As I played, I started to win and had quite a few points on the machine, even though I hadn't asked how much they paid off. I thought that would be uncool.

When I was finished getting my gambling buzz on,

the bartender totaled up the points. She gave me an I.O.U for $120, telling me there wasn't enough money in the drawer to pay me off. I told her I'd stop back and headed out the back door.

Just then Clicquo walked in, bumping into me. He asked how things had gone with the judge. I explained the Keystone Cop scenario I'd gone through, and that the bailiff had asked me for his last name and then assured him I hadn't given it up. I gave him a hug and thanked him for the try.

I went back to the salon, and Bill and I hopped into his Chevy Blazer and headed home to the hood. While we made dinner, I took a couple tokes off a spliff and talked about what we were going to do about Mom's situation. After dinner we were all talked out, so we said our goodnights and I was off to my Lazy Boy chair with the dog blanket in hand and Lil' Dog sleeping on top of me. My only hope was to get a good night's sleep without any gunfire outside. Before nodding off, I thought that Mom's court date for July 9, 2009, would be my last trip back to good ol' Rockford.

The next morning, I was up, showered, and shaved early. Bill dropped me off at the bus, gave me a fist pump, and I was on my way to O'Hare for my flight.

My luggage was quite a bit heavier than usual because I was taking a set of chrome-plated bocce balls back to Aspen. I was sure it added about twenty-five pounds, but I carried it on and they didn't weigh it. As my bags went through the x-ray, my eight balls showed up on their screen. This brought things to a halt. TSA called for more security, and they very carefully took out the wooden box and one by one put the chrome plated bocce balls through the x-ray machine. Then one of the examiners realized what they were. As the people behind me in line got anxious, I tried to reassure the TSA personnel that my balls were regulation size. This brought a few chuckles and laughs. When they finished up, they gave me the all-clear sign with a smile. I was on my way back home.

As Arthur has often done in the past, he picked up at the airport in Aspen, and as always, he had his old, fluffy, white golden retriever/cross-mix dog Snowy with him. As usual, she was unleashed and causing mischief. Like after the last trip, the car ride home was full of me talking like a machine gun and Art digesting every word.

Finally, back home at the cabin on the river, I got on my computer to check my email and to decide on my next plan of attack. I didn't realize what a battleground this seemingly simple court case would become. I found out that I could engage the judge, but only in a family court case with ex parte communication. I started to draft a letter to the judge, who happened to be Lisa Fabiano. It's kind of a coincidence that her aunt, uncle, cousins, and grandparents had lived across the street from my brother's house in the hood when I was growing up.

This brought back memories of when I was a five-year-old crossing the street, which I wasn't supposed to do. The judge's grandfather, who looked like Geppetto in Pinocchio cartoons, would take me by the hand and let me walk through his garden and pick Italian tomatoes. I took those memories out of the letter, not wanting to play that card. I thought maybe my father or my sister had already beaten me to the punch.

The letter was as professional and to the point as I could make it. Having not written a letter in years, it was a struggle. But when I was finished, it wasn't so bad. In it I explained again what my brother David and my father had done since January, 2009, and included the reports that I had obtained.

I realized that, by law, if she did indeed read the letter,

she'd have to share it with the ad litem and my dad's attorney. That wasn't a problem for me, but I wasn't about to send the letter just yet.

When I was back home, I knew there were only three weeks to prepare for Mom's court date. I called Bruce Person, Mom's LCSW, and after a brief conversation, he agreed to testify on Mom's behalf as to her mental state in March 2009. My next call was to my brother Bill and his children to make sure they were on board. So far, all was going smoothly.

Then there was my lawyer, J.F. Heckinger. I left him messages asking him about my status to which he didn't respond. When he finally called back, he asked for Bruce Person's phone number and said that he would send me a draft of his motion for my mother's hearing on July 9, 2009.

Meanwhile, I continued to do hair and tried to keep myself financially solvent. With all the travel and expenses, this journey was draining all my resources and I was losing customers because I was not in town when they needed their hair done.

Bruce called me about ten days before I was to leave and said he would testify. However, he found his conversation with J.F., my attorney, rather odd. He said J.F. didn't talk about what Bruce was to say in court, only that he thought I should give him more money, and further stated that if I did, he'd do a better job.

I found this rather out of line. I've always believed that your business with your attorney was private and protected; I guess not.

On July 1, 2009, I received the draft and a bill from J.F. Reading the bill, I was stunned, but after going over the motion, I was repulsed. He sent me a draft that would all but bury Mom. It was to have her adjudicated, which was the very thing I was fighting against.

I immediately called J.F. on the phone and with a voice that was not pleasant, told him what I thought of his motion, and that I didn't want it filed. I further stated that I believed that what he was charging me for the motion was rather lofty. I didn't spank him for talking with Bruce Person about my bill, but I should have. Finishing our conversation, I told him I'd see him on the ninth of July.

During my time in Aspen, the only connection with my mom was through her two sisters, Phyllis and Marilyn. For some reason, maybe the Mother's Day fiasco, she recognized her current situation and knew that her sons Bill and John were going to great lengths to get her out of the home so she could be a free woman again.

Two days before I was going to depart, my father shut down all of Mom's communication with her sisters. This just crushed both of them. I tried to reassure them that I was doing all that could be done using the legal system, for what that was worth.

The last task I did before leaving was to study guardianship procedures only to find out a very disturbing, but very important fact: whoever files for guardianship first emerges victorious ninety percent of the time. It's wrong and shouldn't be that way, as you'll learn as we continue this saga!

I had another early morning; I was up at four, got packed, and headed to the airport. I hate to fly as it is. However, I've been on over three hundred aircrafts in the last fourteen years, and most trips have been enjoyable. Most of them have been to San Diego to see Robin. But it's no picnic when I have to travel back to Rockford. I can only hope that this one will be my final trip for Mom, and that we get some closure.

After two bus rides and two planes, I was back in the hood, home sweet home. Greeted by the four dogs, I struggled to stay standing with my suit over my shoulder and luggage in hand. I then settled in.

Sorting out my files, all four of them, I noticed they were getting fairly thick, so I jumped in the Blazer and headed to Wal Mart to purchase a Kevlar attaché to carry them in.

Later, after dinner with Bill and his youngest son Matt, I was off to my Lazy Boy bed with Lil' Dog on top of me. I didn't sleep much, just kind of tossed and turned, worrying about stray bullets, lawyers, and judges.

I crawled out of that chair at six a.m. showered, shaved, and dressed down to my Nicole Miller Martini socks, I arrived at court.

As I waited on a bench with the courtroom doors looming across from me, I watched for Bruce Person and my brother Bill to show up. Bruce appeared first, saying he was totally prepared. As we waited together, I informed him that my father had further isolated Mom from her sisters. Bruce just shook his head in disgust and then responded by telling me that he found it highly unusual when my father refused to participate when he interviewed her for competence.

About half an hour had passed, and there was still no judge. Then a bailiff strolled up the corridor of courtrooms, looking as if he could be of some help. When Bruce chirped up that we were there for court with Judge Fabiano, the bailiff said that she wasn't in court that day. We thanked him as he walked off.

Neither one of us had been notified by the courts or my attorney, J.F., so we walked down to the clerk's office where we were informed that the court date had been moved up to July 6, and that Winifred Carol Wyman had already been adjudicated. I wondered how that could be. How could they hold a hearing without all parties present? How could they deny Mom legal counsel or due process of law to have a jury trial, or to present evidence and testimony from her LCWS? I wondered if this happened all the time to other people. It was just so unjust.

Thanking Bruce for his time, I went out of the courthouse to find Bill. My head felt all clouded. Bill picked me up and inquired about what happened, and, with kind of a blank stare, I told him they held court without us. They left the court jester out, me. I was pissed, really pissed.

Having one more stop, I hobbled over to J.F.'s office, only to find out he wasn't around. I left a firm, but friendly, message for him to call me immediately. I told him I was in town for the hearing that had already taken place and would like some sort of explanation. By the time the day was over, I made two more phone calls to J.F., but to no avail.

By that time it was getting late on a Friday, so I got out of my suit and into my civvies, and went off to dinner with Bill and two of his boys. There wasn't much for me to do on the weekend, so I got some needed rest. Then, for some reason, I felt compelled to go to my childhood church and ask the congregation to pray for my parents.

I didn't wear my suit, but threw on my Tommy Bahama dress shirt and my Ray Ban Wayfarer sunglasses and headed for church. Finding the church was fairly easy. It looked smaller than I remembered, but once I was inside, it appeared more familiar. Taking my place in the second pew, I could look in back of me before the service to see if there was a recognizable face. That's when I discovered Bob Aten, who had been a family friend for as long as I could remember.

The congregation had changed to more of a rainbow, one-third black, one-third Hispanic, and one-third white. That was a pleasant surprise. Maybe Rockford was becoming more progressive, I thought to myself.

Another surprise was a female Hispanic minister. As I listened to her sermon, I felt some comfort, even though while I call myself spiritual, I am not a Christian. At some point during the service, she asked her flock if there were any special prayer requests. I raised my hand and she handed me the microphone. Standing and facing the congregation, I introduced myself and asked them to pray for my father to get the help he needed for himself and for my mother, too.

We said our farewells, and then I was off to the hood house to get Bill to go junkin'. We arrived at the antique mall and I hobbled in with my cane. I've got a bad hip from skiing, biking, and other extra-curricular activities, so if I sit too long, it hurts.

While we were amongst all the treasures and junk, Marilyn, Mom's sister, called, sounding kind of sad. She said she wanted to call her sister, but she was on the no-call list. I told her that since it was Sunday, she should just use a fake name and maybe they wouldn't notice the phone number. She thanked me and hung up.

An hour later we were back on the road, done junkin'. About ten minutes later, I received a frantic phone call from Marilyn saying that she had talked to Mom and that Mom had said she'd been beaten up really bad by a strong black man in a wheelchair. She said she had a black eye, bruised jaw, and a knot on her head. We were on speaker phone, and Bill and I looked at each other in disbelief. This big dog was royally pissed, and this big dog will fight if you rattle his cage.

Bill pulled over to the side of the road. Then Marilyn asked if we would call the police. I told her she'd have to call because coming from us, it would be pure hearsay. So she called the police and then called us back when we were almost home. She told us they would have given her a welfare check at Alden Park Strathmoor, but they didn't think it was their jurisdiction. Well, it seemed to me it had been their jurisdiction in May when I tried to remove Mom from the same facility.

Later that evening, Marilyn called Bill's house. The police had made their welfare check, and indeed Mom had been in a boxing match and lost. From the sound of it, she did a Muhammad Ali "rope a dope." They further stated that the perpetrator had been removed for a week, had his medication adjusted, and returned to Park Strathmoor Nursing Home. Mom had been examined by a nurse who gave her a clean bill of health, but she should have been taken to the hospital to be checked for broken bones or a possible concussion. The hospital was only 100 yards away.

I wouldn't find out for another two months when this assault occurred.

It was late, and Monday morning would come too soon. I was mentally spent; that Lazy Boy and Lil' Dog look so inviting, and the next day would be a busy one. I didn't even think about drive-by bullets, and was soon sound asleep.

My routine was feeling pretty normal by then, get up early, give the dogs their slices of cheese, clean up, and go off on my errands. The first stop was the district attorney's office to again complain about the perjury on the orders of protection my father had filed. As I sat in the waiting room, who should appear but my attorney, J.F. Heckinger. He didn't spot me at first, but when he became aware of my presence, he turned with a surprised, almost worried look on his mug with his walrus mustache and blurted out in a voice of disbelief, "What are you doing here?"

I looked him in the eye with a look that could kill, and said, "You didn't tell me not to be." When he heard that, he hurried on through the second door. The receptionist returned behind her thick glass window and informed me that the district attorney wouldn't prosecute my father.

As I headed for my next stop, the thought going through my mind was that apparently, the government only enforced laws on a whim!

Next, I went over to the guardian ad litem, or GAL Her name was Kimberly Timmerwilke. Apparently Ruth Robinson had handed the case to someone else in her office.

Walking in without an appointment, I thought I'd take a chance and catch her at the office which was in the same building as the F.B.I offices. I announced my arrival to the receptionist and she said she'd squeeze me in.

Kim Timmerwilke came in and escorted me to her office. She walked in and the first thing I observed is that she was a very beautiful woman and much younger than I thought. She was nothing like her counterpart, Sharon Rudy, and pleasant enough.

As we talked, I gave her the information I had on the orders of protection, Dad's lying, and the emotional and physical abuse that my father had inflicted on Mom over fifty-nine years of marriage. She then copied the papers I had, including the Bruce Person report.

Then, in return, she shared her information with me. She said she was thrown into the case when it conflicted with Ruth Robinson's vacation at the time. However, since it was her obligation, she had met with my mother and, in her opinion, thought she was delusional when she repeated that she thought she was in the "snake pit." That was the second time I'd heard that. Hmm!

She went on to state that Mom had asked for her own legal counsel and that she was opposed to my father being her guardian. I thought that should've been another red flag and she thought she wasn't serious about legal counsel, which was my mother's right.

I thanked her and she told me to stay in touch if I had any more information. Before leaving her office, I turned to her and told her my mother had been beaten at the nursing home. The look on her face was shock. Apparently she hadn't seen my mother recently, so I still had no clue when the beating occurred.

Traveling over the State Street Bridge, I pulled up to State and Madison, a place where I'd played pool in my younger days. I went next door to Catholic Charities to see Terri, Mom's ombudsman. This time I waited until she came back from lunch, so after forty minutes, I was in her office. I told her about Mom's beating at the nursing home and the subsequent non-existent medical care. Her only reply was, "Your mother was only hit once." I knew better, so totally disgusted, I thanked her and left her office. On my way out, I thought to myself that I should have said, "I don't care if she only got a fist raised at her. That shouldn't be happening in a nursing home." Shoulda, woulda, coulda.

My next drive was to state police headquarters out West State Street. I'd be driving by my brother Marc's gravesite, so I thought I'd stop for some spiritual guidance.

Then on to State Patrol Headquarters. Their offices are about seven miles out in the country, which kind of takes them out of the danger zone.

After parking, I hopped out of the car and went into the office. I was greeted by the shift sergeant with his crew cut and military-type police hat. He seemed friendly enough, so I explained how I discovered "Triad," where multi-government and non-profit agencies work together to stop elder abuse. When I was done explaining my situation to him, he referred me to special agent Sam Thomas of the Illinois State Police, and gave me his business card with the contact numbers. After thanking him, I left to make one last stop.

I thought a little news action might stir things up, so I stopped at Channel 17 television station. I went in with the intention of talking with a reporter, since small town TV stations are more approachable. It's not like walking into WGN Studios in Chicago.

The news director came out immediately, stating that he was busy and only had a few moments, so I gave him my story to date in a nutshell. After all my other stops, I was starting to feel like a broken record. After listening to me, the director assigned a reporter to talk to me. She wasn't there, so he gave me her card. I told him I'd call later and took off.

It was late, so I headed back to the hood, tired, frustrated, and ready for a good meal and, hopefully, a good night's sleep. Tuesday morning would come awfully early.

Up and at 'em. I traveled light, so packed all my dirty laundry and put on that suit again. Then I went back downtown to the Illinois State Police Investigation Office. This time I was in a newer building on the river, the Zeke Georgi Building. It has its own security guards and they check ID's and you have to state your business and then you're in.

This time the door to the Illinois State Police Office was as intimidating as the FBI's. You ring the bell, state your business, and wait for them to let you in. I was greeted by Detective Sam Thomas, special agent, who wasn't wearing a suit, but a shirt and tie.

As we sat in his office, I rattled on about the complete saga as he furiously jotted down notes. As I talked, I put extra emphasis on the orders of protection and how my father had perjured himself, which is a class four felony, and the fact that the DA's office didn't care to prosecute.

Sam listened with a sympathetic ear and promised me he'd look into the situation. Before bidding our farewells, I asked him if he had a mother. He paused for a moment and then replied in a sad voice that she had passed. I told Sam I was so sorry to hear that and that I was sure he understood why I was fighting for mine.

My next stop was across the street to the FBI office to talk with Randy about the skull. I got lucky because Randy just happened to be in the office. As we talked, he explained that he'd been busy, but he asked me how my father would react if he were to question him.

Knowing my dad, I told Randy he probably wouldn't be very cooperative. However, with his disdain for authority, he just might crack. Randy told me he'd keep in touch. We shook hands, said our goodbyes, and I was on my way to my final stop before escaping back to Aspen.

Since I hadn't been in downtown Rockford in years,

it dawned on me that there weren't any drug, food, or retail stores there. There were just a couple of restaurants and art galleries. Other than those few businesses, downtown had turned into a legal community of law offices, FBI, state police, city police, sheriff's office, jail, state attorneys, Winnebago County Courthouse, and a new federal courthouse that was being built. Then it occurred to me, Rockford had been a major manufacturing city, but that had all but disappeared and pretty much been replaced by a legal system driven by money, guns, and lawyers.

My last stop was at my attorney's office. Again he wasn't available. However, his secretary informed me that my next court date would be the twenty-seventh of July. I had a check in my pocket for twelve hundred dollars, but because of his avoiding me, I decided to hold it until he talked to me and explained why the court date had been moved, and why I wasn't allowed to testify.

Then I drove back to the hood, changed into blue jeans and a hoody, fed the dogs some cheese, and went to Bill's shop to pick him up to take me to O'Hare. We chatted and discussed Mom's beating, the courts pulling a fast one by moving the date, and the fact that I'd be back in two weeks. I told Bill it looked like we were in for the long run.

He dropped me off, and after a couple of fist pumps and, "Love you, bro," I got onto the aircraft for yet another escape.

After settling into my window seat, I took out my spiral and grabbed a pen, thinking I'd just scribble down a few of my thoughts. As I wrote, the pages began to fill quickly. It was then that a light went off in my head that would eventually change my life forever. I was going to write a book, a cautionary tale, something that would warn people of what could happen to them if their loved one were in a system which is much less than perfect, one that's corrupt and only cares about the bottom line, not the humanity that the aging process involves.

I decided on the title, <u>Against Her Will</u>, because that's exactly what had happened to Mom. Now, I'd never written anything except for a small diary I kept after my brother Marc was killed in a midair collision in 1976. So I wasn't really sure about how to write a book. I knew it was an art, so I applied what I had learned over the years doing art, pottery, sculpture, etc., and also a lesson I've carried most of my adult life that I learned from my dear friend Paul Soldner, an internationally renowned artist.

Paul would say that in art, as in most things in life, there are no rules as long as you're not hurting someone. Most importantly, you do your art for yourself. So there I was, about to become an author. How good? I don't know. But if my tale, the story, what I write, can help just one other person or family not to have to go through what I'm going through, I think it will be well worth it.

Home again. By now you know the routine. Arthur picked me up at the airport while I jabbered all the way home with him listening, etc. Back at the metal cabin, I left my luggage in the living room because I knew I was going back in two weeks. What a life. If you were to ask me, I think the court system was just trying to break my bank. But I'm stubborn, and wasn't about to give up. This was no longer about my mother's situation; this was a cause and one I believe in fighting for because I'm only twenty-three years behind Mom. I don't have kids, so I've got to look out for myself, and the one way to do that is by writing this book to create change. Otherwise, I'm doomed, as is the rest of the baby boomers, and we just can't let this happen. We need to take action now; resurrect the Gray Panthers. Seventy-three million of us will all be on drugs to wake us up, drugs to put us asleep, and for whatever else they perceive us to have. So we can keep that wonderful machine of nursing homes, lawyers, courts, and big pharma in the money. At this point, I've found that if you follow the money, you'll be able to find the source of the injustice and the corruption.

As I warmed up my computer, I gazed out at the river and wondered if Mom was still being abused at Park Strathmoor. We weren't privy to that information, only that the Rockford Police had done a welfare check on her even though they couldn't figure out if they had any jurisdiction in the nursing home.

Since my lawyer J.F. wouldn't return my calls, I decided to take matters into my own hands. When I Googled the Illinois Department of Health, I got their phone number and was off.

When you call a government agency, be prepared to wait on the phone for long periods of time and to be shuffled from one department to the next. You'll feel like you're on a merry-go-round, but when you finally hit pay dirt and reach the right department, they're ever so helpful.

When I reached the department of nursing home abuse, they were very polite and concerned, taking in all the information I could give them and guaranteeing me they'd do a full investigation. Not knowing what this may or may not accomplish, I had my mother's sister Marylyn do the same, figuring two complaints were better than one.

Before heading back to Rockford, I'd spend the next ten days trying to fit in all my clients. I couldn't afford to lose many more because of my absence.

It's hard to do things long distance, but somehow I

managed. I had Bill go down to get a police report on Mom's beating and my Mother's Day fiasco. They told him no reports had been filed. Now I had some cop friends in my life and most of them don't even like to give tickets out because it creates paper work they just don't like to do. So not having a report on the alleged assault, nor on the forty-five minutes I spent trying to remove her from Alden Park Strathmoor just didn't make sense.

I did as much as possible before I packed for what I hoped would be my final day in court and headed back to the airport for my fourth flight in three months. That's a lot of flying.

You have probably figured out my routine by now, the flights, the bus, Bill picking me up, the hood house, the dogs and, yes, that uncomfortable Lazy Boy I sleep in.

As I settled in, I made a couple of calls before court, to my lawyer, who didn't return my calls, and to Bruce Person to see if he was available to testify. He had just done an evaluation of Mom, and this time she got 27 out of 30 questions right on the mini-dementia test. In his opinion, she didn't need nursing home placement at all, which was court ordered. I thought I had all my ducks in order.

My day had finally arrived, but apparently J.F. had called back to say that his services wouldn't be needed this time, that this hearing was just another status hearing.

Arriving at court, I patiently waited in the courtroom. This would be my first time in front of Judge Fabiano, but not my last. Even with the orders of protection, Bill had decided to go to court with me, but the whole court deal ended up being a waste of my time. I wasn't allowed to speak much, or give the court any evidence I had accrued.

When I did try, it would always be over the objection of my father's attorney, Sharon Rudy. Even more confusing, my lawyer, J.F., did nothing to help.

We left the status hearing, feeling we'd been had. My travel, Bill's presence, Bruce Person waiting in the wings, was all for naught. I think what J.F. had said about his friendship with Sharon Rudy was seen to be true, and it was working against me. This would be the first time I felt they were in collusion.

The first call I made after court was to Bruce Person, the licensed clinical social worker. He told us to stop up and he would explain the evaluation to us. Bruce said he had spent almost two hours with Mom and thought she was more than fine. He felt like he was doing a covert operation and didn't want the nursing home to sit in on his evaluation and didn't' feel a need to give them a copy since I was court ordered to pay for it. He accomplished this quite well.

As he walked us to the reception area, we stopped as Bruce spoke up again, saying that this was where my father had become somewhat angry and defiant, refusing to sit in on the evaluation, which Bruce said would have been oh so helpful. Bill and I thanked him profusely and were on our way.

After dropping Bill off at his shop, I headed back downtown to J.F.'s office, and again he was too busy to see me. He probably should have made some time, since I had that check for $1,200 burning a hole in my pocket. His secretary said she would pass on the information, and also informed me that the next court date would be fourteenth of September.

Then I made my way over to state police headquarters to talk with Detective Sam Thomas. When I met with Sam and told him of my frustration with the courts, he told me he had some bad news. He knew I was telling the truth, but had contacted the District Attorney's office and, for whatever reason, they refused to prosecute. Without the DA office behind him, his hands were tied. Thanking Sam, I was off to the next stop, Kim Timmerwilke's, the court appointed guardian ad litem.

In Kim's office, we had a fairly pleasant conversation. She made it clear that she couldn't, or wouldn't, give me any legal advice. But I was there primarily to give her Bruce Person's report and let her know about my reservations about Sharon Rudy and J. F. Heckinger.

Kim told me she didn't always agree with Bruce and didn't on this. This is when I explained that my mom had always lived in a fantasy world, and made up, or embellished stories her whole life. It's just the way Mom is.

In our conversation, I mentioned to Kim what the Illinois Department of Health was doing and investigating, at which point she stated she had a mother, and if she were me, she'd be doing the exact same thing.

Being a hairdresser and able to talk with women pretty openly, I found out she was a single mother of two lovely daughters and had to juggle her career with being a single mom. With that, I thought to myself that someone other than me does have a heart in this case, even though we didn't agree on everything.

Then I drove back to the hood, got out of my monkey suit, and went down to Bill's shop. Bill still had clients, so I hurried over to the North Main Tap next door, and with martini in hand, I was back at the slot machine. While I was winning, Clicquo walked into the bar. I cashed out and took a seat next to him and filled him on on what happened at court that day.

I then asked him if he knew anybody at Park Strathmoor, and if he thought there was a way to spring Mom out of that prison. I told him I knew what risk I'd be taking, and that at that point, I was willing to do anything, especially after the beating Mom took.

Clicquo said that he'd give it a shot and he'd call me when all systems were "go." I first had to get Bill's approval to take his car back to Colorado and make sure my girlfriend Robin wouldn't flip. But it was my mom and I felt that the risk was worth it.

Bill reluctantly agreed. He knew if I pulled this off that I'd be charged with kidnapping. Robin was another story. She thought I was crazy and stupid and was angry with the whole situation. I thought I'd better rethink this idea.

Bill, his son Matt, and I headed to dinner. The best thing about all those trips back to Rockford was getting to know my nephews again, since I'd been gone for so long. It was nice. After dinner, we went back to the hood. When I finally got the call from Clicquo stating that he was on his way to Park Strathmoor to get Mom, he asked me if I wanted him to go forth. I was silent for a bit, then said, "Abort," explaining that I didn't want him or me to get in trouble, even though I knew if I were caught, I would say I acted alone, an unspoken rule. I thanked him for the effort and said I'd try my luck in the courtroom.

When we arrived back at the hood house, I was pretty spent, so I went off to my Lazy Boy with Lil' Dog for a well-needed rest. I was exhausted and depressed from another wasted trip.

I got up the next morning and packed to go. Bill would drop me off at the bus before work. It was a nearly silent drive. I felt that somehow, by leaving this time, I had failed Mom, that I probably should've snatched her. Anyway, the fistpump, "Love you bro', goodbye, see ya in two weeks," exchange was becoming just a routine.

On the bus, I felt kind of numb and didn't want to write. I just wanted my mind to be blank, if only for a moment.

Once on the plane and settled in, I took out my pen and spiral, and the writing started again. As my thoughts flowed onto the paper, I realized that what I was up against was probably bigger than I. But for the sake of my brother, nieces, nephews, and my aunt, I would continue to make these trips and sacrifices, knowing that Mom's life depended on me.

There would be only two weeks before my next court appearance, and I hoped the Illinois Department of Health report would be in before I went to court. I was hopeful, because, as you know, in all situations in life, "There's many a slip between a cup and a lip."

CHAPTER X

CAROL DOES A HOUDINI

Well, I was finally back home in Aspen, trying to get all my clients in before my next trip. All this court crap was draining my resources, financially and emotionally.

I was only home for two days when the slip between the cup and the lip happened! I was sitting at home about 10:00 on a Friday night with my good friend Jimmy Coates. He was talking about his mother being put in a nursing home by his sister and how helpless he felt when I received a collect call from my brother Bill on my cell phone. I gave the operator my debit card number and started talking to Bill. He told me that Mom had checked herself out of a nursing home up the street from his shop with the help of her hairdresser, Lynda, and he was in Nebraska on his way to Aspen with her. Not wanting to stay on the phone with me too long in case the police were trying to track him, he said he'd call me when he got close.

I didn't sleep at all that night, and by the next day the Rockford Police had left me a message on my cell phone asking if I knew my mother's whereabouts. I wasn't about to return that call until Mom was safely in Aspen and in good hands.

Estimating they'd arrive about 3:30 p.m., that didn't leave me much time. So I called my friend Jackie, who's a licensed clinical social worker, and she agreed to meet me at the Sunday morning concert at the music tent. Aspen has one of the best, if not the best, classical programs in the world for nine weeks in the summer. It was one classical superstar after another with full orchestras, and Sunday morning concerts are free.

I found Jackie outside the tent and asked her to walk to an area where we could talk. We sat down on some rocks by a stream and I filled her in that Mom was on her way to Aspen. I told Jackie that Mom had escaped, and I wanted her at least to check her out to make sure she was o.k.

She thought about it for a few moments, then said she was afraid that if someone found out, it would affect her license in Illinois. I was a bit upset, but I understood it was her career. I then made a quick exit. It was kind of rude, but time was of the essence, and I had so little time.

I went over to the house of a good friend of mine, Roxy, to use the phone to see if we could use Paul Soldner's house as a meeting place. He gave me a green light. Then I called Michael Gillian, who lived in Aspen Village in a trailer he called Rancho Deluxe, asking if I could hide out with Mom there until I knew what my next move would be.

I was almost certain that the police and other law enforcement agencies would be looking for us nationwide. Now that I'd have her, I wasn't about to let her go back to that hellhole where they would drug her and abuse her, not on my shift.

As I made myself as comfortable as possible at Roxy's, I anxiously waited for Bill's call. At that point I just wasn't sure how much trouble we could be in. I also realized that I wouldn't let them take her back, even if I had to barricade myself in some place until I could talk to a state representative or senator or someone with some pull.

Bill's phone call finally came at three-thirty in the afternoon. He'd driven straight through from Rockford, 1,100 miles, in about twenty-four hours.

He and Mom met up with me at a small gas station/grocery store on Highway 82. We both were quite nervous as we drove to Soldner's house. It was a good place to meet, fairly isolated on five acres close to town.

When our caravan arrived, Paul and his caregiver Pam welcomed us like family. They got some food in Mom and some for Bill since they made very few stops on their journey.

Marilyn showed up and was thrilled to see her big sister, and the tears just flowed. We transferred Mom's suitcase, which was all she had, and cleaned out Bill's car. Then he jumped in and left. He hadn't been there for more than an hour. Bill thought the law would be looking for him, so he left and drove straight back to Rockford, twenty-four hours without any sleep.

We then loaded Mom into my car and headed to the safe house at Rancho Deluxe. Mike was ever so helpful and put us up in the apartment attached to the house. The funny thing was that one of the top sheriffs and a friend of mine lived ten feet away.

I called on some friends, and finally, Joy, a long-time friend who would later edit my book, agreed to help me for as long as it took me to set things up with senior protective services and any other organizations I thought would be beneficial.

Joy arrived to give me a hand, and at this point Mom was pretty confused. She was coming down off psychotropic drugs and who knew what else. After running my errands, I returned and Joy left. Mom and I were extremely tired, she from the car ride and I from not sleeping all night due to the anxiety of the unknown.

I hadn't seen Mom since May 11, and she didn't look so hot. She was pale and thin, and had a huge knot on her forehead, a black eye, and bruised jaw. You could tell she'd been beaten. It made me livid to think that the ombudsman Terri had said she only got hit once. It was obvious to anyone that Mom had taken quite a beating. Now knowing this and what the responsibilities of a guardian were, I again was baffled by the court's decision to leave my father in that position. First and foremost, his job as guardian was to keep Mom out of harm's way, which would have involved removing her from Alden Park Strathmoor, the nursing home that had failed to report the assault.

The first night at Michael's was hell. I tried to sleep on the floor, giving Mom the bed, but she was too weak. She made it to the bathroom twice that night, but the third time she was confused and couldn't make it. She stood by the side of the bed and just peed everywhere. Not having raised children, this was all so new to me, but I soon found out that the learning curve is very fast.

Marilyn was getting pressure from the police for a welfare check. She finally gave in, but only under the condition that they wouldn't arrest her, or make Mom go back to Illinois. They all agreed.

They gave us a time limit. We needed to be at Marilyn's house at five-thirty, so I loaded Mom up in the truck and drove down valley to Marilyn's. We got Mom upstairs; then shortly thereafter, two cars pulled up, one white sedan and one sheriff's car.

Marilyn went out to talk to the deputy, again asking him to promise not to take Mom away. He reassured her that this was merely a welfare check.

She led him inside and up to the living room, followed by a rather attractive blonde who was head of senior protective services. Her name was Kim Hildebrand.

Being my usual self, I tried to make the mood as light as I could with small talk. Within a few minutes I discovered that Kim and Sheriff Craig were from the same small town, Homewood Flossmoor, where my girlfriend Robin and also Jackie, the L.C.S.W. I had talked with at the music tent, were from. Small world, isn't it?

Craig went first with his interview. It was short and sweet, and he stated that he was satisfied that Carol was in good hands. He was going to leave, but I convinced him to stick around for Kim's interview.

Kim was much more inquisitive and thorough with her questioning. Since Mom had had about thirty hours of rest, she was very cooperative.

Kim asked Mom how she felt about being in Colorado, and Mom responded that she felt happy and safe and glad to be with family who cared for her. After a few more questions, Kim got around to the beatings she took in the nursing home. Mom was very graphic and described the beating in detail. Then, after she was finished, she said, "What's that matter? My husband beats me too."

We were all silent for a moment; then Kim and Craig said they were satisfied. They thanked us, gave me their business cards, said to keep in touch, and left. What a relief.

We stayed at Marilyn's for awhile and ate dinner. Then it was time for me to take Mom to the metal mansion and to settle her in. I'd cleaned out my bedroom so she could have her own room, knowing full well that I'd be banished to the couch for heaven knew how long.

Mom seemed to like the house. It was a far cry from the cinder block walls in the prison with curtains. It wasn't her home, but it was better than where she'd been.

Since Kim Timmerwilke was the eyes and ears for the court, she'd be the only one I'd call back in Rockford. She seemed sincerely concerned and relieved that I had Mom and that we'd already had the welfare check done. Her only request was that I would get Mom to the hospital for a physical check. I replied that I'd do that immediately.

Within the next half hour, Mom and I were on our way to the E.R. at Aspen Valley Hospital. They took us right in and a doctor's assistant started to take Mom's vitals. Everything was fine with the exception that she was extremely anemic. When the E.R. doctor arrived, I had him examine her head to make sure her jaw wasn't broken, another thing they hadn't done at Alden Park Strathmoor. He said her jaw was fine, but he did note the golf ball sized lump on her head, the black eye, and bruised jaw. He also gave her a short version of the mini-dementia test, and stated that she wasn't too bad.

Then I asked him if there would be any adverse effects if she came off psychotropics cold turkey. He said she'd be okay, but if I saw any sudden changes, to bring her back in.

Mom kind of liked the attention she was receiving from the young doctors. I didn't remember at the time, but it came back to me later that Mom always reacted better to men.

Having that out of the way was a relief for me also, so on the way home I put another call in to Kim Timmerwilke, telling her that Mom went to the hospital and had a mini-physical, and except for being extremely anemic, she was just fine. I told her I'd keep her informed of any changes and would see her on the twelfth of September. I told her I was working with social services in Pitkin County, Colorado, and that I intended to keep her here. She did not object, but before she said goodbye, she suggested I get Mom an internist.

Like I said, I never raised children, and all of a sudden, I had elder teenage-mother to care for with little or no experience. Except for what I learned from Grandpa Howard when he took care of Grandma the last three years of her life.

I also had to learn to juggle my time so I could get clients in, as it was touch and go if I were to make enough money to keep things going.

Another one of my guardian angels was my roommate Arthur, who always picked me up after my trips back to Rockford. Arthur also had his dog Snowy living with us. She's a medium Samoyed/golden mix and just the mere fact that Mom had a dog with her made her function better.

Arthur would turn out to be a great help. Since I worked during the day, either at home or on the road when Mom could go with me, and Arthur worked at night at home, I could sleep at night and Arthur would do the night shift in case Mom needed something. It wasn't perfect, but it would have to work, and it did.

Through social services, the next step was to find an internist for Mom. I was referred to Dr. Goyette and Dr. Scheuer. We ended up with Dr. Ann Goyette.

On our first visit, I sat in on the interview. It was

at that time that I noticed Mom was agitated by all the questions. It was only later that I realized she was tired of all the prodding and probing. Add that to all the medications the doctors in Rockford had prescribed, and she ended up with a basic mistrust for most doctors, especially female ones.

Since Mom had been locked up and isolated for four months, it had to be quite an adjustment for her. And with her living with me, it definitely changed my lifestyle.

Was Mom perfect? No. Was she ok? Yeah. Was she dependent? Somewhat. At that time, I hadn't explored nursing home abuse very much, but what I discovered very quickly was that institutionalization teaches learned helplessness which leads to feelings of entitlement. These were obstacles I had to learn to reverse, which was not an easy task.

What Mom wanted most of all, desired most, was to be outdoors. I don't think she'd seen the sunshine since May 11, 2009. Through the generosity of my good friends Scott Martin and his wife Kathryn, Mom received a cement bench so she could read and write in the backyard outside my salon window. She was so happy she'd sit outside for hours.

Mom's backyard bench was short lived, though. After about a week of sitting on the bench, during our usual routine of dinner and getting ready for bed, she called me into the room and, with her leg propped up, showed me her knee. It had an odd-shaped red mark, almost like a curling iron burn. Then Mom dropped a bomb, saying she'd been bitten by a spider and her leg hurt like hell.

For the ten days she'd already been with me, she hadn't complained much, so I took her very seriously. I loaded her into the car and drove directly to Aspen Valley Hospital. I checked her in, still using the power of attorney she'd signed in May, not knowing if it was still in effect. But it was all I had.

Since the wound didn't look very bad to the nurse, we were put in a little cubicle to wait. After an hour and a half, the doctor showed up. His name was Bud and I recognized him from around campus/town because living in Aspen is like being in a college that you never graduate from.

Mom and I explained that she'd been bitten by a brown recluse, to which the doctor replied that that was impossible; there were no brown recluses in Aspen. He thought it looked more like a scrape from a fall. But I interjected that the scrape was on top of her knee. So with that, Dr. Bud put on some Neosporin and a Band-Aid and sent us on our way!

By Monday, Mom's leg was looking a lot worse. The good thing was that she had her first physical with her internist, Dr. Ann. She was a young doctor, kind of pretty, but not all that cheerful. I left during the physical part of the exam. Afterward, however, I had Mom hike up her pant leg and show Ann the spider bite. Again, I was assured that it looked more like a scrape than a bite, but she told me if it got any worse to come back.

On Thursday morning of the same week, after Mom's shower, she sat on the edge of the bed, hiked her skirt up, and showed me this scab that was two inches long, one inch wide, and was concave about a quarter inch. So Arthur and I loaded Mom into his Chevy Blazer and drove back to the doctor's office, this time without an appointment. Dr. Ann had a day off, but her partner Kim Scheuer was there. She was young like Ann, but a lot more cheerful.

She took Mom into an exam room with me following, and as soon as she pulled Mom's pant leg up, she gasped and said, "Your mom's been bitten by a brown recluse, and its poison is still eating her flesh." She went on to say she'd have to remove the scab. Now this was no little scab and was set in a way that I couldn't see how she could just pull it out. So I left the room and let her have at it.

Hearing Mom yell all the way in the waiting room, I knew the deed was done and that Dr. Kim had pulled the scab off. I went back in and she showed me how to take care of and heal the wound. She prescribed some antibiotics and some silver sulfadiazine cream to dress it. She explained it could take a couple of months to heal, and she wished that we'd caught it earlier. I just thought to myself that I tried, but was glad that the third doctor, Kim Scheuer, was educated enough to recognize it before it was too late.

Dr. Ann and Dr. Kim received Mom's blood test results, and with what knowledge they had about her gastric bypass and the blind loop syndrome it causes, they referred her to Dr. Ira Jaffrey.

Between working on clients and juggling Mom's appointments, we did slip in some fun. We'd go to concerts at the music tent on Sunday mornings and meet up with my artist friend Paul Soldner and his caregiver, Pam. They'd have us over for dinner a few times before Paul went back to Claremont, California for the winter. Mom and Paul became fast friends since she'd worked in clay most of her adult life. They would just chit chat back and forth while Pam would give me subtle tips on care giving.

The second time we went to dinner, Pam made her version of shepherd's pie. It was delicious, and since Pam is from England, I think it's the only national dish they do right. But the most humorous part of the evening was when Paul put his hand on Mom's leg. I couldn't stop laughing. There was my mom, whom I hardly know, and one of my best friends of thirty years was putting the move on her. At my age, I was glad to see that we can still have strong libidos into our eighties.

We were on our way to Dr. Jaffrey's office in Glenwood Springs. It's about a seventy mile round trip, and regardless of the weather, we would make this trip once a week for the next five months.

We met Dr. Jaffrey in his office, which is located at Valley View Hospital. He's a nice older Jewish doctor who had just turned seventy, not much younger than my mom. I explained again how Mom had escaped, about her gastric bypass and blind loop syndrome and he promptly figured out her course of treatment, iron shots and B-12 once a week to get her blood levels up.

In the course of the conversations he had with Mom, at one point she stated that she had been in the "snake pit." Without hesitation, Dr. Jaffrey said, "Oh, you mean the movie starring Olivia de Havilland, where she's put into an asylum against her will."

I was floored. I'd told Mom not to tell people that because they'd think she was delusional. Boy, was I wrong. Then it dawned on me. There we were with a doctor from her generation who knew exactly what she was talking about. Up until then, they'd all been younger and hadn't understood what she was referring to.

As I'm writing this, I'd like my readers to think outside the box. We baby boomers, whom I refer to as the disposable generation, need our peers to evaluate us, because those youngsters who are professionals have no idea what we're talking about.

Dr. Jaffrey and I had a good relationship. He'd always have a Yiddish joke for me and Mom when we went to see him. One time I gave him pictures of me having lunch with the prime minister of Israel, Benjamin Netanyahu, saying, "Here I am with a world leader, but I can't get my mom out of her adjudication in a small city in Illinois."

On our trips to town, Mom always would worry that we'd see a police car. After three welfare checks called in by my brother David, for who knows what reason, she was scared that they'd take her back to the "snake pit." I'd just tell her, "Over my dead body."

David called one more time, so I made the usual arrangements and met with Officer Hugh Zucker of the Pitkin County Sheriff's Office. He got out of his car, walked up to Mom's passenger window, and did his interview. Then I explained what was going on and said what I'd done for Mom up to this point. He responded, saying that most of the sheriff's department was aware, and they told David to quit calling, that there would be no more checks. I think Mom was relieved.

After Hugh's welfare check, I decided to take Mom to the mental health building to see Peg McGavock. She runs Response, which is a hotline and agency for battered women and men. Peg's been a client of mine for twenty-some years, and was glad to see Mom and me.

Mom would go on to explain in detail her beating at Alden Park Strathmoor, and I just wanted Peg to see her injuries while they were still visible. We had a pleasant conversation, and as we left, she told me to call her if I ever needed anything. Peg would become one of my closest confidants.

Part of my newly appointed job was going through and trying to organize Mom's drawers. It was kind of awkward for me, her grown son, to be putting away her bras and panties, but while I was doing this one day, I came across her diaries. Until that moment, I didn't even know they existed. Mom saw what I'd come across and encouraged me to read them. So after feeding her and settling her in bed for the evening, I lay on the couch and started to read them.

What I discovered while reading the diaries was that Mom had kept a fairly clear and accurate account of her daily activities and thoughts while she was held against her will. Reading them, however, was extremely upsetting. She would date each page and explain who she saw that day, such as her son Bill, grandson Goobs, or my father, and what they would bring her on their visits, mostly Diet Coke and Hershey's chocolate. This would make her happy, but she would always plead with them to take her home, even my father.

Mom even kept notes on her visit with her first guardian ad litem, Ruth Robinson, and how she told Ruth that she wanted her own legal counsel before her hearing on July 9. Ruth's only response was that after the ninth of July, everything would be a piece of cake. But she didn't say for whom. This just enraged me more, especially since the hearing had been moved up to July 6, two days after her unreported beating. Mom also described that in detail in her diary, which made my blood boil.

As I went on reading, Mom described how she was sexually assaulted on June sixteenth, that two men had entered her room at Park Strathmoor and started masturbating on her bed. As I read on, Mom stated that maybe she'd just rent out her bed. That made me think to myself that Mom was going to become a prostitute.

But in the very next paragraph, she went on to write that she'd find someplace else to sleep. That made me laugh.

She also went on to say that the nurses forced her to take her medications, which she didn't like because they made her feel weird, and she'd often palm her pills.

One particular entry was from her stay in the psychiatric ward at Swedish American Hospital. When my sister Beth visited her, Mom threw a bedpan in her direction because Beth told the nurses Mom was suicidal. Mom stated that she never said that, but she did say that she'd rather be dead than to live like that, being medicated against her will.

As the days went by before I was to return to Rockford, I received the report from the Illinois Department of Health. The report only reconfirmed my conviction for having Mom's adjudication overturned. The story in her diary and the one from the state were identical, but Alden Park Strathmoor failed to report the beating and its severity, even though they were very aware of it. The man, who was a patient, hadn't hit Mom just once, he had beaten her about the head. It made me sick, but I could hardly wait to bring these documents to court and settle this once and for all.

By this time I thought I was getting the soccer mom thing down pretty well. However, Mom and I did have this ongoing fight about her wearing granny panties, or Depends, grown-up pull-ups. I'd have to say that wearing them would be pretty demeaning, so I didn't blame her and finally gave in, only to realize she didn't need them anymore. I discovered that when you're raising an adult teenage daughter, you'd better pick your disagreements carefully.

I'm leavin' on a jet plane, my carry-on getting much heavier due to the legal documentation I've accrued. How nice. This was my fifth trip in as many months and the first time I'd left Mom home with Arthur, my roommate, and my Aunt Marilyn. It would be my first break from Mom in six weeks, and I have to add that even though it wasn't a pleasure trip, at least it was a break.

CHAPTER XI
ME A LAWYER? NOT!

Another flight, a bus ride, and I was back in Rockford. I was afraid to say it, but it was starting to feel like home. Ain't that something? I wasn't too happy about being there again, and I could only hope that it was my last time for awhile.

Back in the hood, I slipped into my Lazy Boy with Lil' Dog and tried to get some restful sleep. I was appearing in court the next day, and I felt extremely confident that all my ducks were in a row. Brother Bill had my suit dry cleaned, and everything was in place, or so I thought.

Bill and I got ready and drove down to his barber shop for what I hoped was my last high and tight lawyer-looking hair cut. I dressed at the shop, hopped in his Chevy Blazer, and we were off to the court house. It was almost feeling too natural for me to be in downtown Rockford. I spent quite a bit of my childhood there, and about ten months in beauty school when I was seventeen.

Parking the car in the lot for my lawyer's office, I decided to go on into his office and wait for him. It was all locked up, so I took a seat on the stairs and I waited. Then I remembered that I'd left his check for twelve hundred dollars in the car, so I scooted back to the car, then over to the courthouse and waited outside the courtroom for J.F. to show.

Since we hadn't planned to meet, it made sense to wait at the courthouse. Mom's guardian ad litem, Kim Timmerwilke, showed up first, so after I greeted her and gave her the reports and other information on my mother's well being, she slipped into the courtroom.

Next to show was my father's lawyer, Sharon Rudy. Until this time, I'd only had a glimpse of her. I kind of expected my father to be in tow, but he was nowhere around. Ms. Rudy just strutted right past me, as if I wasn't there. I just took her visual appearance in. She was short for her weight and in comfortable shoes and walked with a rather masculine gait. She was in need of a hairdresser and looked tough. But I was certain that I had enough hard evidence to turn this case around.

Nine-thirty a.m. was court time, and there was no J.F. in sight. I wandered in and took a seat. Five minutes passed and then J.F. Heckinger came flying into the courtroom. He walked so fast that his tie and suit coat were flowing back as if he was standing in a wind.

At about this time, the judge, The Honorable Lisa Fabiano, walked into the courtroom and things seemed to start moving extremely fast. I was still sitting in the gallery when my lawyer asked the judge if he could approach the bench.

J.F. talked so fast that I could hardly understand him. As he rambled on, he basically asked to be dismissed from the case due to the fact that I didn't communicate with him and he hadn't been paid. At this point, my mind was whirling. I had my phone records with me which would prove that he hadn't called me back, except once, and all my calls to him were documented. I couldn't believe my ears.

Without even asking me if this were true, the judge let him step down. Sitting there stunned, but thinking quickly, I told Judge Fabiano that was fine, but I could not afford more legal counsel, so I'd have to go pro se. From all my research on the computer, pro se wasn't bad, or for that matter, unusual, in family court, since it seemed that it's supposed to be a little more relaxed when a plaintiff goes pro se.

Kim Timmerwilke went over and retrieved a pro se form for me, and when I started to fill it out, J.F. blurted out, "Don't put down that you're an attorney!"

I just slowly glared up at him and turned to the judge and said, "What do I put down, a hairdresser?" With that, J.F. flew out of the courtroom as fast as he had arrived, not looking at me or saying that he'd see me later. Even though I still had a twelve hundred dollar check in my pocket.

I finished filling out the pro se form and handed it to the clerk. I was told to approach the bench, where I found myself in front of a female judge, with a female bailiff and two female lawyers on either side of me. There were no other males in the room, but having been a hairdresser for so long, I was comfortable around women.

I was able to speak first, and it felt great since it was the first time I was able to be vocal since this whole fiasco had started. Without being told what to do, I spoke first, not about the evidence I had, but about Mom's journey, her emotional and physical health, and most of all, her joy and happiness caused by not being locked up and drugged where she didn't belong. I thought the judge and Kim Timmerwilke were somewhat impressed by what was being done for her by her middle-aged son. They smiled.

I then asked if I could present any evidence, to which

Ms. Rudy objected right away. Judge Fabiano looked down, and proceeded to tell me that since I just went pro se, there would have to be another court date. Acknowledging that this was probably getting quite expensive for me, she asked me when it would be convenient for me to return.

I thought that was awfully kind of the judge and replied that around Thanksgiving would be acceptable, since I could kill two birds with one stone and have Thanksgiving with my girlfriend Robin and her family in the suburbs of Chicago. The other parties agreed rather reluctantly, saying that the 30th of November was so far off, but realized that I'd been back to Rockford five times in as many months.

Judge Fabiano and Kim Timmerwilke also agreed that my mother was in good hands and was safe. The fact that they felt that way still baffles my mind to this day, because if Mom was all they said she was—homicidal, suicidal, and demented-- then why was a son with little or no experience able to do a job that took a whole staff at Park Strathmoor to do? These were the very people who put her there at a cost to taxpayers of six to seven thousand dollars a month. I thanked the judge and the ad litem Kim and left the courthouse with what I felt was a partial victory, no thanks to my attorney.

As I started to drive away from the courthouse feeling somewhat relieved, I started thinking about my former lawyer's behavior in court and how he treated my case from the beginning. It was then that I realized that his initials, J. F., stood for Just Fucked.

My next stop was downtown at the Illinois State Police Office to talk with Detective Sam Thomas. He was there and able to see me. I asked him about the District Attorney's reluctance to file charges against my father for perjury. He looked down, than back up at me, and explained that without their cooperation, his hands were tied. I understood what he was saying; however, the state police and the DA's office were supposed to work together as they are both part of the Triad Organization. I guess it only works on paper and in theory.

Before leaving Sam's office, I filled him in on how my mother was doing in Colorado. A smile came to his face and he expressed his happiness for me. With that, I thanked him for trying and was off to my next stop.

I drove across the river for a few blocks and stopped in at Catholic Charities to talk with Kathy, who is head of the ombudsmen, about my conversation with her underling, Terri. I also wanted to give her the Illinois Department of Health report of Mom's beating at Alden Park Strathmoor and their negligence in their failure to report.

I told Kathy about my encounter with Terri when she'd told me my mother had been hit only once, and I interjected that I didn't care if only a fist had been raised against her, or if she had been only threatened. This shouldn't happen to anyone in any nursing home. I told Kathy that I hoped she'd talk to Terri about doing her job better.

Kathy thanked me for my concern and information, and for taking care of my mother so well, and she said she'd have a talk with Terri about the incident. I wasn't trying to get Terri in trouble; I just wanted her to be put on notice to be more thorough at her job, so that doesn't happen to someone else's family member.

Next, I headed twenty minutes north to Bruce Person's office to give him an update on Mom and to give him a payment on the court ordered evaluation. Bruce was extremely pleased that Mom had the self determination to escape. However lucky or unbelievable the story, he was glad she was finally safe.

Thanking Bruce for his time, I told him I'd see him in November after my next hearing to see if he'd be able to testify. Since my next step would be to have Mom's adjudication set aside, it was adios, then back to the hood for a well needed rest. It had been a long and eventful day.

Bill was home with his youngest son Matt, sitting in the living room. After going upstairs and changing, I came back down and went out on the back deck of the house to smoke a spliff and listen for gunfire. It was another Saturday night on the west side.

After a couple of puffs off the joint, I put it out, then walked back into the living room to fill Bill in on the day's events. Before I could speak, I looked at Bill and he was as white as a ghost. I asked Bill what was wrong, but he didn't respond right away. When he did, he said that Shane, or Goobs as we call him, Bill's gay, twenty-one-year- old son had just gotten home from being with his boyfriend and as he sashayed across the living room on his way to the basement where he stays with his mother, he said, "Dad, my ath is on fire." With that, he disappeared downstairs.

Not knowing what to say, for some reason I blurted out, "You know, those boys play rough!" Bill didn't find my comment very humorous, so I sat down to console him, saying that I understood that whether it was a son or a daughter, a father just doesn't want to hear that.

When Bill finally settled down, we talked about his fears of having a gay son, even though I thought of Bill as a liberal redneck. His fears were that Goobs would get AIDS, or worse, that he'd be beaten up by gay bashers like Matthew Shepard had been in Wyoming. I told Bill I understood since I had met Matthew's mother at a book signing in Aspen during Gay Ski Week.

We finally had dinner, talked about my day in court, and then it was off to my Lazy Boy, Lil' Dog and a good night's sleep. I hadn't been asleep for an hour when Bill's oldest son, Marc, blew into the house, waking me with the dog alarm system long enough to say good-night.

Marc hadn't been upstairs for more than about ten minutes when all of a sudden gunfire rang again outside, close to the house. Knowing the drill, I couldn't hit the floor fast enough, and with phone in hand, I called Marc upstairs and said that they were shooting outside the house. His only response was, "Welcome to da hood, Uncle John. Get a good night's sleep." So I crawled back into my chair and eventually went back to sleep, not to be disturbed again that evening.

The next morning, after dropping Bill off at work, I had a day off and took off to the cemetery on West State where my brother Marc is buried to clean around his grave marker. On the way, I stopped to get some water and a soda. I was still in the hood, but I couldn't figure out why people, mostly black people, were looking at me funny, kind of with anger or distrust, but I just shrugged it off.

When I was done with visiting Marc's grave, cleaning it up a bit, and having a little conversation with him, I headed back to Bill's. I gathered some things together, and as I was backing out of the driveway, I looked down Winnebago Street to the south. About a block and a half away I saw two to three hundred black people walking up the street towards Bill's house. I didn't know what the crowd was doing, but being the only white family in the neighborhood, I wasn't about to stay and find out.

I drove pretty fast to Bill's shop. As I started to explain what was happening by his house, he simply turned the TV on to the local news. It showed the crowd, which was a horse drawn funeral procession led by the Rev. Jesse Jackson. The funeral was for a young man who had been shot three times in the back by the Rockford Police. He was unarmed and was only wanted for questioning on a domestic violence issue. His name was Mark Anthony Barmore. His shooting had made national news and throughout my journey, the story of his death would parallel my own journey.

When Bill was done working, we jumped in his car and headed to Zammuto's Dairyette on the Southside, catty-corner from the Italian Catholic Church in a hood a little worse than his. It was an unwritten law that no one messed with the church, the Italian grocery store, the Dairyeette, or Maria's restaurant down the street. If someone did, it would be trouble for them, so it was a rather safe corner.

The Dairyette had become black-owned, even though it still carried the Zammuto name. The food was strictly soul food, except for the Italian ice they still served. After ordering pulled pork, fried okra, and a lemon granita, we sat and waited for our food.

We were the only two white people in the place, and it was small. There were about seven or eight black people there, some adults and some kids. As we sat there, I noticed a hefty black woman with a tattoo on her arm that said, "Black Hood," in English scroll lettering. She just stood there and glared at me, not saying a word. You could have cut the tension in that small room with a knife.

As we sat and waited, a gangly little black boy about eight years old kind of danced over to me, sat down next to me, looked up, smiled, and said, "Yo' not really the popo, are you?"

I was taken aback for a moment, then reached up, took off my hat, and said, "Oh no, five dollars at Seven Eleven." It was a black hat that said POLICE on the front. With my short haircut, I probably looked like one. As I spoke, you could literally hear the tension leave the room, and my comments brought more than a few chuckles. Just then, Bill and I grabbed our food and went to eat it in the car.

While sitting there, we ate and had a laugh about the hat. Bill had given it to me when he brought Mom out. When he stopped on his long journey to Aspen, he'd put the cop hat on the dashboard so no one would mess with the car or Mom. As we talked, I showed Bill videos I'd taken on my phone in June of the gangbangers dancing in the street. He just looked at me and said, "What were you thinking?"

I replied, "I guess I wasn't," but I felt safe in my old neighborhood.

As we pulled away from the Dairyette, Bill stated, "If you're gonna wear that police hat, you might as well put a target on your chest." I agreed and never wore that cop hat in Rockford again.

Anyway, we drove back to the house, and I got my stuff together for another early trip back to Aspen. A good night's sleep, no shootings, our usual farewells, one bus, two planes, and Arthur picking me up in Aspen. I was back home safe and sound. Nice.

CHAPTER XII

WHO TURNED THE LIGHTS ON?

Well, it looked like I had my hands full, going pro se in court, taking care of Mom, cooking, cleaning, and keeping my house in order and my clientele together. It was quite a load! It kind of felt like going to school full time and working full time. Whoa!

My only free time seemed to be spent burning the midnight oil. That was when I found time to write and research laws and Mom's medical conditions on the computer. I had to research Mom's conditions because my father hadn't turned any of Mom's medical records over to his lawyer, so I could figure out what help she would need. I had to start from scratch. Here again, the courts could have made addressing Mom's health issues and well being a much easier task. But it was starting to dawn on me that this wasn't the court's first concern. Since the order of protection was still in force, I couldn't call my Mom's guardian who still happened to be my father. This made my life ever so difficult.

Something I hadn't done yet was to do a background search of my former attorney, J.F. When I did settle down to my computer late one night and punch in his name, I was surprised, but not that surprised. The first site my computer led me to was the Illinois Bar Association, which contained a record of J.F.'s license being suspended for six months for using his client's money for his own purposes. The next site was called The Syndicate, which would show if J. F. Heckinger had any mob connections. Bingo, there they were. Apparently, he'd done some shady land deal for three to four million, with some shady partners to purchase an office building that they ended up renting to the Illinois Attorney General's office (Lisa Madigan). I was only hoping that that didn't become a connection for J.F. to keep me from my investigative work for Mom or my book. I didn't know.

I also discovered at that time that J.F. and Dad's attorney, Sharon Rudy, had both worked for and/or had been on the board for Prairie State Legal Services, the organization that I supposed was the A.C.L.U for little people, or people of no importance to them, since they were the organization that referred me there. How convenient for J.F. and Sharon. Things were starting to fall in place. I was finding out that they probably had had the ability to shut a lot of doors for me in Rockford. So much for that.

The best thing about my not having court for six weeks was that it enabled me to take a trip out to California to see Robin for a week. That would be good, because she was becoming somewhat impatient; she hadn't seen me since March of '09 and really needed her hair done. However, I had a few more projects to pursue before I departed.

One of the first projects I had to do was to see if I could obtain legal counsel for Mom in Colorado. Upon inquiring, I was referred to Alpine Legal Services. It's located in the Mental Health center in Aspen. I loaded Mom up and made the drive seventeen miles up valley. We went into office where we were met by the legal director, Bill H. I explained Mom's situation with the courts in Illinois to Bill. He put his chin in his hand and paced back and forth, trying to get a bead on what I was looking for, and if he could help.

I told him I'd like to have Mom's adjudication set aside in

a Colorado court. However, I had read that once adjudication had taken place in another state, the original state from which said judgment was handed down had absolute control over the ward.

I found, and I think anyone in their right mind would find, this fairly new law to be absurd, especially when that court and the social services of that state happen to be eleven hundred miles from here. With all the evidence as to the way Mom's case was handled in Illinois, the courts might take a look. But that's not the law, and it's my belief that when someone physically moves, the jurisdiction should move with them.

Bill ended up being absolutely useless. In fact, he turned into a gadfly even to the point of accusing me, unbeknownst to him, in front of some of my friends, that I was just an old Aspen drug dealer. These comments raised the hair on the back of my neck. Here is another lawyer, who, after I confided in him, would make such a statement.

I made sure to nip that rumor in the bud and got word back to Bill H. that he should watch what he says. Hell, I grew up some in Aspen in the wild years and would be a liar if I denied doing any drugs. In fact, there was a joke out there that if you partied like a lot of us did in Aspen in the 80s and 90s, you probably snorted at least one condo up your left nostril. But if I'd been a drug dealer, I'd probably own a house on Red Mountain, an exclusive community, and own some commercial real estate besides. So I knew he couldn't be speaking of me, since I live in a trailer in the barrio. Catch my drift?

Against Bill H.'s advice, I went ahead and filed three restraining orders in Pitkin County, Colorado, against my sister, my brother David, and my father. They made sense to me, and Peg, who worked for the Battered Women's Program thought it couldn't hurt. But the Judge Erin Fernandez rejected them, saying that the people who I was filing against lived too far way. I thought that was odd, since the one filed against me was good in all fifty states and Puerto Rico. It just didn't seem fair.

While I continued to take care of business, I still found time to take Mom down valley forty miles to see Dr. Jaffrey. Mom still didn't seem right. She was coming off the psychotropic drugs and the therapy for her blind loop syndrome was a slow process. But she was coming along mentally the best she could.

Finally the day had come. I was off to San Diego to see Robin and all the gay friends I'd inherited over the years. You see, Robin's a "fruit fly," which means that most of her friends are gay men, and after thirteen years of dating her, they were my close friends, too.

On the way to the airport, a routine I'd repeat for the next year, Arthur would drive and we'd take Mom and Art's dog, Snowy, with us. Aspen is so laid back you can bring your dog into the concourse when you drop people off. It's cool, not like any place I'd ever lived. After our goodbyes, it was up, up, and away to California, hopefully to relax and get some more writing done.

I wasn't on the ground for forty-five minutes when I received a frantic call from Arthur. I was sitting in the waiting room of Robin's eye doctor where we'd stopped on the way home from the San Diego Airport to pick up her new glasses. So not to be rude, I stepped outside to talk.

Art filled me in. Apparently, a couple of hours after I'd left Aspen, Mom started to complain about chest pains, and he wanted to know what to do. Since Mom had lived with me for almost twelve weeks, I knew she wasn't a complainer.

I told Arthur if she didn't need an ambulance, to go out to Highway 82 and then right, not left, and take her to Valley View Hospital in Glenwood Springs. This ended up being a good choice since I'd already had a bad experience at Aspen Valley Hospital with the missed diagnosis of the spider bite.

Back at Robin's, I called Arthur to get an update. By this time, Mom's sister Marilyn was at Valley View Hospital with Art, waiting for the doctor in the emergency room. After that call, all I could do was wait patiently.

Robin and I went to dinner at C-Level, a restaurant on the bay with good views and, as usual, a warm night in San Diego. After a phenomenal meal, we went back to Robin's and sat out on her beautiful patio with a stream flowing in the background. How peaceful.

I finally received a call from the E.R. doctor at the hospital. He started off by asking me some very peculiar questions, like was I feeding her, and had she been to a doctor recently. I responded by stating that she had, and then explained her gastric by-pass and blind loop syndrome and how she came to be in Colorado. The doctor said she was short two pints of blood, not very good since we only have about five. He said he'd keep me informed and asked permission to give Mom some blood. I gave him the go ahead and informed him of my power of attorney that should have been on record. I thanked him and then it was off to a California king-size bed and a good night's sleep. No couch tonight!

The first thing the next morning I called the hospital. I reached the nurse on Mom's floor and she informed me that they'd keep her a few days. They'd given her two pints of blood and fluids to rehydrate her. She went on to say that that much blood loss would have to happen over a long period of time. I told the nurse that Mom had seen a doctor every week since she arrived in Aspen, including the welfare check-up at Aspen

Valley Hospital, and at least five different doctors had stated that she was extremely anemic. It was then that it came to me. She was probably two pints short of blood when she escaped from Rockford, and if she hadn't escaped, she probably would have died in the nursing home due to blood loss. Once again, it was Mom's cognitivity and self-preservation that saved her life. Isn't that something?

I didn't cut my trip short, especially since Mom was in the hospital for a couple more days. It just wasn't necessary. So Robin and I spent the extra time talking about Mom, doing my honey-do list, and having a great time. Still, the trip out to San Diego was just too short.

On the way to the airport, heading back to Aspen, Robin and I talked in the car about how long I'd have Mom. Robin told me what a good thing I was doing, and she was happy to see what a good caregiver I was. Since she has M.S., after thirteen years of dating, she could see that I'd take really good care of her. If her disease eventually takes its toll on her, I'd step up to the plate and be her caregiver. It's funny how that works, but it does.

At the airport, it was hugs and kisses goodbye, and I was off for more airplane rides. Back in Aspen, I was surprised to see Arthur, Snowy, and Mom at the airport to pick me up. I hadn't expected Mom to be there.

On the ride home, Mom talked up a storm. This was different from the first month and a half. She remembered things from before the transfusion, but now she was like a superstar as she continued to yak. It was like someone had turned the light back on. She wasn't perfect, but almost whole again. She was getting the needed oxygen to her brain. What a relief. She was running on all six cylinders; she never had eight.

Now I had a mom who could think on her feet. Her humor came back, but with that she also realized she missed her kids back in Rockford. It was then that I explained to her that she couldn't go back until I figured out the court case. But life went on. In the ensuing days, Mom told me she wanted a piano, wanted to paint again, and started attending church. That's a lot for a woman who was just existing for the last six months.

Mom had told me when she arrived that she wanted her mother's piano and her personal belongings that she'd left in Rockford. I told her I couldn't get them until I went back to court and asked for those items. However, I told Mom that I had loaned my friend Donnie my piano and that he said I could have it back.

I waited until Mom went to Marilyn's for dinner one evening, and then gathered the boys, Piano Pete, Frank from Rancho Deluxe where we first had Mom when she arrived on August 1, and Arthur, along with his trailer which had no back lights or plates. We wanted to move the piano before Mom returned home.

The job was accomplished just before Mom arrived. I don't know how four fifty-year-old men got that piano through the fence, over the hand rails, and into the trailer, but we did.

The piano ended up in the kitchen, and when Mom finally came in and saw it, her eyes lit up like a child's on Christmas. All four of us guys got warm fuzzy feelings as Mom sat down and gave us a concert, playing a few songs from memory. Boy, what a sight!

For the next few days, Mom would play every morning. My crazy friend Biff, who has his degree from USC in music, traded music lessons for haircuts. Biff, who is kind of wild looking, with hair like Rod Stewart's and always off the wall, had fun giving Mom lessons, and playing and singing for her. It wasn't because of her attention span, but the lessons were short lived. Her real love was visual art; she really just wanted to paint.

In between taking care of my clients, keeping house, etc., I made time to purchase art supplies: canvas, acrylics, brushes, and palettes. So with a donated easel, Mom started to paint. It was like I created a monster. We'd give her a picture or image of something, and Mom would duplicate it with her own twist. From Georgia O'Keefe's flowers to Van Gogh's "Starry Starry Night," this would be some of the best art I'd ever seen her do over the years. And she was doing it so late in life; it was a gift.

Since Arthur rented out his trailer, he'd be helping me out through the winter, so we had him and Snowy the dog living with us. So there I was, cooking three to four meals a day, cutting hair when I could, and making sure all of Mom's needs were met. Since the transfusion, she was one hundred percent more cognitive, to the point that she'd occasionally cook, but I'd never eat it. I never liked her cooking.

With her new-found state of consciousness came some rebellion, especially at bedtime. She got in the habit of wanting to paint in the middle of the night. I'd learned to pick my battles, so if she wanted to paint, no matter what the hour, so be it. Anyway, I'd just heard a piece on NPR on some elders in New Jersey that didn't want to sleep at night, so someone started a program where they'd pick them up at ten p.m. and take them to a hall to dance, socialize, and have a good time until the wee hours of the morning. Then they were returned home, where they could sleep all day. I thought that was a great idea; let them live the way they wanted, not how other people wanted them to. So I used that rule with Mom.

Another one of Mom's great loves was the theater. She had been very involved back in Rockford with the "New American Theater," the Mendelssohn Club, and the Coronado Theater. So it was a good thing that one of my best friends Jimmy, who, on my suggestion, became an aspiring singer/actor, had the lead role in an upcoming play, The Wiz.

Jimmy needed a coach, and Mom would become an exceptional one. Jimmy, who worries why Jell-O wiggles, would come over with his mother's dog, Genie. He inherited the dog when his sister placed his mom in a nursing home against her will. Jimmy couldn't do anything about it; his sister pretty much had her own way.

My mom would hold the little long-haired Chihuahua and read scripts with Jimmy, coaching him to say his lines with rhythm, as if he were singing. Jimmy finally got it, and Mom would attend his play three times, once with a friend of Jim's and mine, Mary Sue Bonetti, without me.

She was so proud of him.

There would also be dinner at my house with Mary Sue, her father Bill, Jimmy, and Susan, a good friend of mine. This was a scene we'd repeat many times in the next five months. Mom also started going to the Eagle County Senior Center twice a week on Tuesdays and Thursdays from 9:30 until 3:30. It gave us a needed break from each other.

Then there was a new client and friend, Clem, who is truly a southern gentleman. He is about my age, but has a father who is much older than Mom. His father lives in northern Florida and has a really sound mind. He does his crossword puzzles and Sudoku. Clem feels kind of guilty that he only goes there twice a year, so he offered to take Mom to lunch to make up for his unwarranted guilt.

During the next few months, Clem and Mom would have lunch two or three times, and they both really enjoyed it. It would be these acts of kindness from friends like Mary Sue and Clem that would help foster Mom's full recovery.

There were other friends, too. Kathy Sovich, an RN friend who specialized in elder care would help me with Mom's pills and be there for me throughout my journey. Sandy Holmes, the nutritionist for the hospital, would advise me on Mom's diet. Friends like these, money just can't buy. They are all truly genuine, and I couldn't have accomplished what I did without them.

And then there was my long-time friend John M. I'd know John for almost twenty-eight years, starting when I did his and his family's hair. John sort of looked like and reminded of the brother I had lost in a plane crash.

John got caught up in the pot business in the 80s and 90s, and he'd gone big. Some of John's stories were incredible, scuttling boats, having boats sink, and landing planes at clandestine strips. He was very cavalier, a bit like Ted Turner. But the law caught up with John through the CCE Act, years after he retired from the biz.

John would receive thirteen years. During that time, we would become closer. I'd send him books and even see him two times while he was incarcerated. He would teach me more about institutionalization, which proved to be very valuable information for me during my mother's recovery, and for that I'm ever so grateful.

I'd done everything I could imagine before my next court date, so I'll have to share with you my return to church before my next chapter. It was a no-brainer for me to decide which church to pick. It was The Prince of Peace church at the entrance to Aspen.

The church was built by the Mennonites, so it was well-built, and the denomination was Methodist. I knew the pastor, Greg Anderson, and his girlfriend, Carolynn. So for the next seven months, we tried to make that forty mile round trip journey on Sundays.

On the first Sunday we went back to church, Rev. Anderson and I looked at the walls almost in unison, and said "I hope the walls don't fall down." Mom and I settled in to the back pew, lest I fall asleep, and for the second time in a year, I was about to sit through another sermon.

When Rev. Greg was finished reading the scripture, he began his sermon, and I was pleasantly surprised when he started speaking. His sermon was on Oktoberfest and its origins. It started as the celebration of crazy King Ludwig's wedding, a party that lasted three weeks. It was such a great party that the tradition turned into a festival in Bavaria which is still celebrated to this day.

Then Greg went on to talk about the prayer bread, which is how we got the shape of the pretzel. In those days, instead of praying with their hands palm to palm, they crossed their arms across their chests, hence the shape of the pretzel.

After the service, the congregation was ushered into the courtyard of the church where their own festival was set up. Imagine that, there I was, at ten-thirty on a Sunday morning, drinking beer, and eating brats and sauerkraut. Looking around, I didn't see many males, and I thought to myself that if they knew what went on in church, there'd be a much larger congregation.

The next week at church they had communion, and darn, if they didn't use real wine. I didn't participate, but

Mom did.

On the ride home, however, I would pop a cork for the first of three times, and go off on Mom. You see, Mom has a little problem that she's had for as long as I can remember. She takes things that don't belong to her and then lies about it. This has little or nothing to do with her cognitive level. It's just something she's always done.

Mom had taken a pair of earrings that my dental hygienist, Kelly Keefe had left on my station when she'd had her hair done. Mom had squirreled them away and put them in a plastic box which she proceeded to hide in the hood pocket of her winter coat. I discovered the earrings in a small plastic box there, and when she lied about it, I pulled the car over to the side of the road and chewed her out.

Afterward, I felt really stupid. Here I was, a grown man, reaming out his elder mother. Ain't I the asshole?

The highlight of all the services was that they always had an art gallery showing the fellowship room in the basement of the church, and we'd go down for coffee and treats after worship.

This particular Sunday, they had a new photography exhibit. As I walked around looking at the photos, I came across a three foot by five foot black and white photo of a nude. I paused for a moment, then realized that I recognized the girl in the photo. It was tastefully done; however, it was a full frontal view. Except for a wisp of hair between her closed legs, she was hiding nothing. From that moment on, I referred to the church as the Church of the Closed Vagina.

On the way home from church that day, even Mom made comments on the nudes. There was also one on the opposing wall who I knew as well. I thought to myself that I hadn't been to church in years, and oh, how it had changed. With them serving beer, wine, and naked girls in the basement, why weren't there more men in the congregation? Oh, well.

Anyway, it was time for me to head back to Rockford again for Thanksgiving and another court hearing. With half a dozen letters from doctors, nurses, and other health care professionals in hand on Mom's greatly improved condition, I was sure that I was more than ready for court. So it was back to da plane, da plane.

CHAPTER XIII

HAPPY? THANKS? GIVING?

It was Thanksgiving week and I was on my way back to Illinois for my first hearing pro se. However, this trip was slightly different. I got to do the fun things first. When I left the Chicago airport, I took a right instead of a left, and hopped the subway (the "L," as they call it in Chi-Town) to the State Building. Then it was a three block walk through the underground chasms of the building to catch the Metra train at Randolph Street Station.

I was either early or late, depending on how you looked at it, for the train. Having about fifty minutes, I slipped over to the bar overlooking Millennium Park, where they had the victory celebration for Barack Obama. Nice view.

I arrived at the Homewood Station at about four p.m., and Robin was there to pick me up. I think I sort of surprised her by not talking about my mother first, because the big news that fall was Tiger Woods' cougar number fourteen on his list.

You have to understand that financially, I had started to live hand to mouth. I was housing three people and feeding two; I was broke. But even though I did Tiger's cougar's hair for about three years, and she made no bones about dating him, the only people I mentioned it to were Robin and her middle nephew, Ben, who golfed. Of course they didn't believe me at first, but when the news came out, they changed their minds. When I asked Robin why she didn't believe me, her only response was that he seemed like such a squeaky clean family man. She just didn't want to believe that about Tiger.

Women tell their hairdresser everything, and I learned not to talk out of school, but the reason I brought the Tiger thing up first is, whoever ratted Theresa out got a huge lump of cash, and oh did I need cash. But that isn't how I roll. Too bad; I could've used the money.

Later, I got a good night's rest and got to spend some much needed time with my princess. We mostly talked about what my plan of action in court would be, but also about her health and all my friends back in San Diego.

Robin finally got her hair done. She had waited for me for six months to do it, and that was not like her, but we have a secret pact. That night she made her mother's traditional candied yams while I watched her. I enjoyed that because I think it's the best thing she knows how to cook. Tomorrow can't come too soon. It's Thanksgiving.

I spent Thanksgiving with my Jewtheran family, half Jewish and half Lutheran. It was a nice mix. There were Jewish prayers and Christian prayers, covering all the bases for the families in attendance.

There was the usual chit chat at dinner; everyone was catching up on what they'd been up to. The boys talked about their schooling, our health, vacations, the usual stuff. And of course, they all asked about my mom and my court case. I gave the family an abbreviated version, so I didn't dominate the conversation at the table.

After dinner, I stood up and gave my shock toast, not realizing at the time how profound it was. "Here's to all my favorite 'F' words," I started. Then I watched as the worried looks came over the adult faces, and Andy, Ben, and Sam, my three teen-age nephews, snickered. I continued, "Friends, family, fate, forgiveness, and forever." They all chuckled. It's a great toast, and one that would help carry me home on my journey.

After watching some Thanksgiving football with the men, we snoozed off. Robin then informed me that it was time to go home to get ready to head back to Rockford. The next morning, I was up early and took the train, subway, and bus back to Rockford, back to the hood.

Before going to Bill's house, I made a quick stop at the courthouse. After talking with the court clerk, I realized that my former lawyer, J.F. Heckinger, hadn't filed a motion. So I did what I thought was the stupidest thing I'd done to date, and that was to file the motion based on his draft which I had rejected. I carefully hand-wrote the whole draft out, word for word, and filed it. Even though I didn't want to file it, that motion would prove to be one of the most important documents in my book to prove collusion between J.F. Heckinger and Sharon Rudy.

It was all systems go, and Bill and I arrived at the court for a nine-thirty hearing. In court, though, that didn't mean it started at nine-thirty. In fact, it didn't start until the real attorneys were there. Kim Timmerwilke then came up to me and informed me that we had to wait for Ms. Rudy. It looked like we were on "Rudy time."

As we sat and waited, I turned to Bill and whispered some James Spader lewd comments, like in the TV show Boston Legal, about the guardian ad litem, Kim. Bill told me to hush. He thought they might hear me, so I quit.

As Bill and I sat and listened to the other cases until eleven o'clock, Ms. Rudy finally made her appearance.

It would be another hour before we were allowed to approach the bench.

I stood in front of the judge with Bill. Sharon Rudy was to the right of us and Kim Timmerwilke was on the left. I was allowed to speak first.

Again, my first concern was to report on my mother's health and general well-being. I explained how she'd arrived in Colorado extremely anemic and was two pints short of blood. It was another point showing that Mom wasn't getting the proper medical care at Alden Park Strathmoor. Next, I informed the court that I had Mom enrolled in senior services in Colorado. Federal programs, however, require a United States ID, which she didn't have.

At that point, Judge Fabiano ordered Ms. Rudy to obtain the Social Security Card, an Illinois ID, etc. It was a court order. Next, I handed the judge the Illinois Department of Health report on Mom's beating, over the objections of Attorney Rudy. This really bothered me, but I bit my tongue and thought to myself, "Isn't the guardian, my father, supposed to watch out for her welfare, even in a facility?" Anyone who'd seen my mother could tell she'd had her face beaten and it was in the report, yet they did nothing.

Ms. Rudy went next and immediately started a personal attack on me, saying that this case had only gone on so long because of my contemptuous behavior. I didn't understand this because I hadn't been charged with contempt. As I had witnessed in the other court hearings, Ms. Rudy's first and foremost concern was who would be responsible for her fees. Not once, or ever, did she ask about my mother's well-being. I really found that odd. Every website I saw on the computer on Sharon Rudy had her as a champion of elder rights, doing pro bono work on state committees that study elder rights and speaking at other organizations to protect elder rights and due process of law. Somehow she must have lost her way, because what Sharon had done, with the help of the courts, was to trample all over my mother's rights.

I asked to speak again and informed the courts that even though I'd been asked for my phone number by Ms. Rudy three times, my father still hadn't called his wife. Then Ms. Rudy informed the court that my father was in a nursing home in poor health. At that point I was starting to realize that the attorney Rudy ran Judge Fabiano's courtroom, or the judge was naïve, obtuse, or involved. I didn't know.

Before we were dismissed, brother Bill, who had been standing there for over forty-five minutes without speaking, did something I wouldn't have the balls to do. He took the picture of the woman lying in her own urine on the floor at Alden Park Strathmoor and flipped this 8 x 11 inch print on the judge's desk, and abruptly made a hasty retreat. With the same respect I'd shown the court since this case started, I thanked the judge for her time. I was then informed that the next status hearing would be January 7, 2011.

Outside the courtroom, I caught up with Kim Timmerwilke and simply asked how Sharon Rudy could make those objections in court, and furthermore, how could she call my behavior contemptuous. Kim's only response was that she couldn't help what Sharon said. Again, I thought that this was family court and it was supposed to be open and gentle. At that point, however, I felt that Ms. Rudy was treating me like some sort of criminal.

With that, I was off to find Bill. I was sure he had left the courthouse after handing the judge that picture. Bill was waiting for me outside the courthouse. I thanked him for being there and tossing the picture to the judge. I was just hoping that the shock of that photo might get her attention. I didn't know.

After Bill dropped me off in the hood to change out of my suit, I waited for my gay nephew, Goobs, to get ready for work so I could pick up Bill's car. Goobs got into the car, and it was the first time I'd ridden with him. I was a little nervous, since he'd just gotten his driver's license at twenty-one and he'd just rolled his boyfriend's truck. He didn't know how to back up, except in bed, or so I assumed. I couldn't help asking him why he'd come home when I was there in September and waltzed through the living room and said, "Dad, my ass is on fire."

Goobs looked at me with his girlish look and replied, "Uncle John, I'm a pitcher, not a catcher; furthermore, I don't even like ath play. But every time I eat jalapenos, my butt burns." With that said, I think I laughed all the way to Bill's shop, wondering whether I should tell Bill, just to put his mind at ease, or let him read about it in my book.

I couldn't keep it from him that long, so I told Bill the story that every time Goobs eats jalapenos, his butt burns and he can't go to work. This put Bill's mind at ease, and we all had a good laugh.

Before I left Rockford, I decided to mail the letter to the judge ex-parte, hoping to get her attention. They must have thought I was doing a great job, even though they've deprived Mom of her social security check, which is a violation of federal law. I would say I was doing a pretty good job myself. So it was back to Aspen and I was glad I didn't have court until January. See ya next year, Rockford.

BEFORE

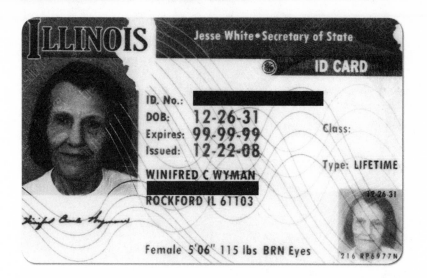

AFTER

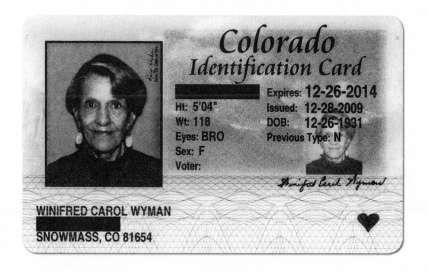

WHAT A DIFFERENCE A YEAR MAKES

CHAPTER XIV
SO THIS IS CHRISTMAS

So now Mom, this person I hardly communicated with during the last twenty-seven years, has lived with me for about five months. In this time I've seen steady improvement in her life skills and in her ability to take care of her personal needs. And her paintings are just beautiful. I must be doing something right.

Then the cougar got a Cougar. Mom had more than a little trouble getting into my '82 Ford F250 pickup. In fact, she had to use a step stool. So I bought a 1996 red Cougar on time from my good friend Roxanne. It cost more than I could afford, but Roxy is pretty lax, and I did pay her off on time. It had rear wheel drive with studded tires. I wasn't sure how it would handle the winter driving conditions, but it made Mom's life easier, and mine.

With quite a few things on my agenda before I had to return to court in January, I began to work on getting Mom her Social Security number, Colorado ID, marriage certificate, birth certificate, etc. So far, the courts had done nothing to help this process; why would they start now?

It took quite a bit of research by Bill and me and many mailings of documents back and forth. It was a big pain in the ass, but by late December, Mom was a Colorado citizen. She was so happy to have some identification; it made her feel like she existed again. She didn't understand the adjudication, and next to the death penalty, that's the worst possible thing you can impose on a US citizen.

Mom finally received her first Social Security check. It was for only six hundred and some odd dollars, but it was a big relief. Until this time, I had supported Mom with little or no outside help. I was the payee and Mom would have to cosign her check. This would be a problem later, but not one we couldn't overcome.

So during the Christmas season, Mom spent her time painting and making Christmas decorations, even going so far as to decorate my ficus tree with the help of Arthur, our roommate. She even made big red bows for all the windows. This was different for me; I hadn't decorated in fourteen years. So this was Christmas.

Mom would also go to the senior center during the holidays. She'd made friends there easily, but after the lunches, she didn't want to hang out and play Bingo. So she would ride on the senior van for a couple of hours and just take in the scenery. She said it gave her ideas for painting landscapes.

Then Brett, a friend of mine who would later design the artwork for my book, brought Mom an easel and sat down and drew with her. Painting sitting up made her paintings even better. Mom was in a state of grace when she was creating.

It was a snowy December, and we still made those weekly trips to Glenwood Springs to see Dr. Jaffrey, no matter what the road conditions were. It amazed me how dat car do dat. I mean, deep snow, slush, or ice, that Cougar just plowed right along, no problem. It was the first car with rear wheel drive I'd ever driven in the mountains. What a trip.

One night, Roxy and Jimmy took Mom and me out for a special treat to see a jazz concert of Billy Holiday music.

The singer looked and sang just like Miss Holiday, and her pianist was off the charts.

When the concert was over, Mom made a beeline for the pianist. She was a stout woman with hair like Don King. When Mom finally reached her, she took the pianist's hands in hers and held them and said, "Those hands of yours are a gift from God." The lady smiled and thanked Mom ever so graciously.

As usual, I was very busy during the holidays, seeing clients at the salon in my trailer and making numerous house calls. If Arthur wasn't home, or awake, Mom would sometimes make the long trek to town with me. Most of the time she'd sit in the car and read while I was doing a client's hair, but on occasion she'd come in and sit there while I worked, watching me and joining in the conversation.

On one occasion, we made our way up to an exclusive neighborhood on Red Mountain to Marion and Don Weiss, two of my favorite clients. They're from Louisiana, and spend summer and winter in Aspen. They are a few years younger than Mom, so being Mom's contemporary, they communicated with her just fine.

Marion and Don knew what I was going through, and Don, being an attorney, knew constitutional law. He looked over my case a bit and reassured me that I was on the right track and that Mom's rights had surely been violated. Even though he wasn't an elder law lawyer, he knew his constitutional law, and after a quick review of my case, he got a look of disgust on his face and just shook his head. For me, this was reassuring as I continued my journey through the corrupt judicial system in Rockford.

I was really busy the week before Christmas, and my

clients that came to the house during lunch would always bring food or baked goods for Mom and me. It was amazing. These random acts of kindness reassured my faith in people.

Nancy B. was one of my lunchtime customers who always brought pizza. It got to the point where Mom would ask when Nancy was coming. She liked to converse with her and loved her pizza.

By this time, Mom had been with me for over five months and kept getting healthier, both mentally and physically. So by now, my clients were all ears, and as they listened to my saga, they interjected their own stories of elders in their families. They told stories of similar problems and abuse, especially when it came to medications. It eased my mind to know I wasn't alone in the elder mess, and also, we're the next generation headed in that direction. In no way is our government preparing for the onslaught of baby boomers, all seventy three million of us. If we don't take action now, it may very well be the largest unnatural disaster this country has ever faced, financially and morally.

Finally Christmas arrived. This would be my first Christmas in thirteen years without my princess, not a good thing. But as Robin always said, when you can't do anything about a particular situation, "It is what it is." Huh, such great words of wisdom.

So Christmas Sunday arrived and Mom was chompin' at the bit like a child to go to church. She got ready, putting on her make-up and Saks Fifth Avenue dress which was gold and lace that we bought at the thrift store for twenty-five dollars. I did her hair, and with her Sorrel snow boots on, we were off to church in a blizzard. In our fancy clothes and our snow gear we were quite a sight.

Christmas services, like Easter, are my favorite. There's

not much preaching or scripture. No naked girl photographs, or beer or wine. Just a lot of very loud classical music, mostly Bach, with an exceptional organist and choir. In fact, Jimmy Coates, my actor friend, sang in the choir and this made Mom so proud since he's like another son.

After church, we trekked on home in the blizzard. The house was warm and we had a few presents under the ficus tree that were sent by Bill and his children. Mom took a seat on her couch as I went to the kitchen to prepare dinner. She soon fell fast asleep, leaving me in solitude, which, for me, was always welcome.

As I cooked dinner, my mind wandered back to Mother's Day and how my father had prevented Mom from being with her children and grandchildren. It just broke my heart when I thought about it and that it didn't have to be this way. She must feel like a foreigner in a strange land in Colorado. She should be in her own home back in Rockford, doing her thing for Christmas, but that was just not to be.

Instead, she had fallen asleep on the couch in her fancy dress at the house of her estranged son, a man she hardly knew, but felt safe with. This in itself brought tears to my eyes as I woke her for Christmas Eve dinner.

I looked at Mom and said, "I couldn't have helped you unless you helped yourself, and you did that by escaping on your own." She just grinned. And I thought, to myself, "So this is Christmas." Wow!

CHAPTER XV

HAPPY NEW YEAR, MOM?

New Year's Eve 2009 turned out to be one of my most memorable ones. In past years, I was either working in a salon or making house calls for the big bucks, doing some movie star, prime minister, Saudi prince, or some notorious person's hair. But not that year. It would only be my usual run of the mill great customers. Oh well. I guess I'd been out of the loop too long, since taking on the mission of making Mom healthier and spending most of my time working out of my salon at home in my trailer.

After finishing my last customer in town, I couldn't wait to get back down valley and home before all the craziness of the celebration in Aspen started. Ya see, this town goes all out for New Year's. If you hadn't had a reservation for a hotel or restaurant for a year, you were S.O.L. You didn't get to play. There was no parking for your car or your corporate or private jet. It was absolutely insane. Aspen is one of the wealthiest communities in the world. In younger days, I'd have stayed in town and taught rock stars how to party. But I've done that rodeo before.

This year was gonna be different. I hopped into my red Cougar and joined the grid-locked mass exodus out of town. It would be a long drive home, so a trip that usually takes twenty minutes was about to take an hour. I put in a CD, lit a spliff, and got in line. Oh boy. After about ten minutes in traffic, I received a phone call. It was the sheriff's department saying that Mom had called "911." She was o.k., but I needed to get home. Getting little information, before I hung up I told the officer I'd be home as soon as possible.

Knowing the sheriff was at my house was a big buzz kill. I had been looking forward to dinner and a nice quiet evening, and couldn't possibly think of any reason Mom would have to call "911." I didn't obsess, but I was a little puzzled.

As I meandered down Highway 82 in a snowstorm, my mind wandered to New Years gone by. I remembered Mick Fleetwood at a small club that only held three hundred or so patrons, or Bruce Willis and his band. We danced all night. And parties at the house of Ted Field of the Marshall Field fortune. It was a great crazy time to be in your 20's, 30's, and 40's. Oh, the memories. Anyway, my mind snapped back to reality as I turned into Lazy Glen where I live, made the corner onto my street and saw three law enforcement vehicles from two different jurisdictions in front of my place. One was from the town of Basalt; the other two were from the Pitkin County Sheriff's Department. I thought to myself, "This is going to be interesting."

I parked the Cougar and headed inside the trailer to a warm refuge. There I was greeted by a Basalt cop and a county sheriff named Jesse. He was in charge. Mom sat quietly on the couch while Jesse filled me in. He explained that Mom had borrowed a phone and dialed "911" from the senior center where she had lunch twice a week. She said her son John had stolen her money, and that law enforcement had to respond and follow up on the domestic calls. I started to explain the situation with Mom to Jesse, but he interrupted politely and assured me that the sheriff's department was well informed about Mom's journey to Colorado and handled her with kid gloves, but also with the respect and dignity she deserved.

I'm sure there were more important duties those officers could have been doing on New Year's Eve, but they let Mom know they took this matter seriously. The officers checked out the house thoroughly, starting in Mom's bedroom, her bathroom, and then the kitchen. They even went so far as to check out the refrigerator. Upon returning to the living room where Mom and I were sitting, Jesse took a seat on the arm of the couch and stated to Mom that the place seemed very safe. The house was warm, the laundry done, and the refrigerator was full of food. Furthermore, it was obvious I'd given up my bedroom because I was sleeping on the couch. He was trying to reassure her that she didn't have it so bad.

Even after all that was said, Mom still wondered why, after she cosigned her Social Security check, I hadn't given her the money. Jesse then turned to me for an explanation. I simply told him our financial situation and that I kept receipts for where the money was going. At this point he explained to Mom again that she was safe and being well cared for.

Mom agreed that she felt safe, so Jesse, handing each of us his card, told us to go on with our evening and to feel free to call him if there were any other problems. I thanked Jesse and the other officers for their concern, and then he asked Mom if she had any more questions. Mom immediately piped up with, "Where's my money?" With that we all kind of chuckled. I assured Jesse I'd explain it to Mom further. So after forty-five minutes or so they wished us happy New Year and were off for a long night.

With the house somewhat back to normal, I made dinner and then explained to Mom how that check was spent and that it seemed that every time she called the police that I knew of, it didn't turn out very well for her. The last time she did that she'd ended up being put away against her will. She agreed and went off to bed for, hopefully, a good night's sleep.

After that incident I had Mom's checks automatically deposited into my account. I didn't want to do that circus again. And we didn't.

Finally, that evening, while my roommate Arthur and Mom were asleep, I was able to catch up on the news in the local papers. The front page headlines read, "Actor Charlie Sheen Arrested Christmas Eve on Domestic Violence Charges." He was accused of roughing up his wife and holding a knife to her throat and had hired a local dirt bag attorney that I didn't care much for. So my brush with the law paled by comparison. Lucky me. As I started to fade from my long day, all I could think was, Happy New Year, Mom!

CHAPTER XVI
BACK TO THE HOOD, "BRR!"

Well, there I was again on a plane headed back to the hood in Rockford, and boy, was January in the Midwest cold. And I mean cold, brr. On the plane to O'Hare, I pondered what lay ahead of me in court. My legal papers and evidence took up two attaché cases and were kind of heavy. My only wish was that I might finally get to present my case without interruptions. I didn't know.

I spent another night in the Lazy Boy with Lil' Dog, and I didn't know how, but I got a really good night's sleep in that chair. I was up early the next morning, and after a fast shower, was off to Bill's for another short lawyer haircut. Bill and I talked about what was going on with Mom and my strategy in the courtroom. He was pretty adamant about not attending for fear he'd be charged with contempt for tossing the picture of the woman lying in front of her chair on the floor in her own urine which Goobs, his son, had taken at Alden Park Strathmoor Nursing Home. So I had to go it alone. It would have been my preference to have some support, but if not, it wasn't a problem.

Arriving at the courtroom early, I sat and waited patiently. The same scenario unfolded. Kim Timmerwilke showed up and asked me to step outside the courtroom where I filled her in on Mom's well being, since she was Mom's guardian ad litem. Then we re-entered the courtroom to wait for my father and his attorney, Ms Rudy. While waiting, I listened in on the case at hand and witnessed a woman being taken down by two bailiffs for contempt because she wouldn't listen to the judge when she told her that her time was up. As they handcuffed her and took her away, Ms Rudy strolled into the courtroom without my father. That's when I realized this family court business wasn't so friendly.

I approached the bench and stood with Ms Rudy to my left and Kim Timmerwilke to my right. I was much more comfortable in my skin this time, and I was allowed to speak first. As I rambled off what had happened to Mom, I told about the spider bite, the sores on her leg probably caused by the medication they had her on back in Rockford, and the methods we used to heal them. I also talked about how she arrived in Colorado short two pints of blood, and explained how neither my father, brother David , nor my sister had tried to call Mom. Ms Rudy made a strong objection to the last statement. I looked up at the Judge and she was smiling, and I can only assume that she was smiling because I was doing such a good job with Mom.

Then I asked if Ms Rudy had obtained Mom's driver's license, Social Security card, and other forms of ID that she was ordered by the court to obtain. It was unbeknownst to her that I'd already made Mom a Colorado citizen with voting rights. Ms. Rudy suddenly started to stammer, almost lost for words, that she hadn't obtained the documents that were ordered. In fact, she stated that she didn't understand the order.

I then informed the court that I'd taken it upon myself to do the necessary paper chase and had obtained the documents myself in Colorado, and I told them it wasn't an easy task. I then thought to myself that Ms Rudy was in contempt of court by defying a court order. It was then that I realized there were two sets of rules, one for them and one for me. If they made a mistake, it would just be a formality.

However, if I broke a rule, I'd be violating court orders and would be held in contempt. Not a level playing field, ya think?

I started to speak again, asking when I could present my case. Suddenly, without explanation, I was cut off from speaking and Ms Rudy and Ms Timmerwilke asked Judge Lisa Fabiano for a side bar. I didn't know what I did or said; it could have been my request to present evidence of Mom's mental health. When the attorneys returned, they had decided to give me guardianship of person. This really threw me for a loop. It wasn't that I wanted guardianship; I wanted it dismissed or set aside. But it would finally legitimatize me and take Mom's heath care powers away from my father. I guess it was better than nothing.

Then, as I stood before Judge Fabiano, she stated that she had to ask me a few questions before she swore me in. She asked if I had ever been convicted of a felony, or had one expunged, or been involved in a domestic violence case or drug rehab. I answered all with a firm "No." At some point during the further questioning, the judge asked me if I'd ever been in jail for anything. I replied with a slight smile, "Yes, once for contempt of court." The judge looked at me with almost a laughing smile. I think she thought that was funny. I did. Then she swore me in as GOP.

Then Ms Rudy had her turn. She started by saying that my father wasn't there due to his poor health. In fact, he was in a nursing home near his sister's in the Aurora, Illinois, area. She also asked for my phone number again since she had misplaced it. I thought to myself what bullshit. It was on record since I'd given it to the police once and to her in court twice. I couldn't understand this behavior coming from a so-called professional lawyer. Then, as she had done the two previous times in court, Ms Rudy asked the judge for financial relief, saying it was my behavior that had caused the case to continue and that I should be responsible for some of her fees. She didn't seem to care how my mother was being taken care of, and I found that odd, since she was the public guardian, appointed by the governor for two counties. It was her job to watch out for the well-being of people like Mom. It just didn't make sense. From the start of these court cases, Ms Rudy's only concern, as far as I could see, was how she was going to get paid. I didn't feel the least bit responsible, especially due to the condition in which Mom had arrived in Colorado.

Before being excused from the courtroom, Ms Rudy further informed the judge that she'd be filing a "rule to show cause" as to why I should be held responsible for her fees. Whatever.

Relieved that I was out of court, but only partially satisfied with the results, I headed back to the hood house to change into my civvies, and then drove to Bill's shop. Again I filled Bill in on the court proceedings and the hollow victory. I also described how they swore me in at court for Mom's guardianship, but told me I'd have to come back in mid-May to complete the transition and receive my letters of guardianship. What I didn't understand was when my father filed for emergency guardianship in May of 2009, it was immediate, and now they were going to take an additional four months to make me official, even though I'd been doing all the things a guardian is supposed to do. This delay and another court date, like most of this case, just didn't make sense. When I was done filling Bill in, he told me he wasn't surprised by this because his own divorce case in the same court had taken over eight years. All I could think at that point was that this was the way Ms Rudy raised up her fees with unnecessary delays. I guess that's how they roll in Rockford. Not good.

I left Bill's, hopped in the car, and headed back downtown to see Kim Timmerwilke and Randy at the FBI I slipped into Kim's office first. I didn't have an appointment, but after telling the receptionist why I was there, Kim agreed to see me. After I was directed to her office, she invited me to sit down and stated that she didn't have much time to talk. I began by filling her in on Mom's mental state. She agreed that my obtaining guardianship was a good move and that she was the one who proposed this to Ms Rudy.

She went on to tell me that even though she didn't agree with Bruce Person on all the evaluations of Mom, if it were her mother, she'd be doing the same thing I was doing. This gave me a warm and fuzzy feeling, but also left me with questions. If Kim could see though all the bullshit that had happened to my mother in this case, and said that she'd do the same thing, then why wasn't this expedited in court? It made me wonder what the duties of a guardian ad litem were. They're supposed to be the eyes and ears of the court, but somehow I thought they must be silenced in the judicial community in Rockford. If Kim was doing her job properly, then whatever she was telling the courts was falling on deaf ears. I truly believe she was trying to do the right thing.

Before I left Kim's office, I informed her that I was writing a book, a cautionary tale of my experience through this labyrinth of the court and healthcare systems. I told her that she's presented in the book somewhat favorably because I agreed with eighty percent of what she'd done. But the twenty percent she was ignoring still bothered me. I told Kim I hoped she would read what I'd written so far as it could prove to be very helpful for her.

She thanked me and wished me good luck on my book and told me to keep in touch about Mom's recovery. So I thanked her for her time, which ran over by about twenty-five minutes, and then I slipped over to the office next door to talk with Randy from the FBI.

Well, that must have been my lucky day. Randy was

in and agreed to see me. I guess I was batting a thousand. We sat in the bullet-proof reception room and talked about the location of the skull, and again he asked me what I thought my father's reaction would be if he were to confront him. I told him my father had a certain disdain for authority, but would probably crack under pressure if he had something to hide. Randy went on to say that he had a friend in the sheriff's department who could use the site where I found the skull as a training experience using cadaver dogs and taking core samples out of the lot vacated by the house. However, they'd have to wait until spring because the ground was frozen. When we were finished talking, I thanked Randy again. Then I went back to the frigid air outside, slid into the car, and drove off to Bill's house.

After a family dinner with Bill's children and some chit chat about how Mom's case was going, it was back to the Lazy Boy and Lil' Dog for some sleep. Ahh. I did find a little comfort from the freezing weather. For some reason there was no gunfire.

I slept so well Bill had to wake me so I wouldn't miss my bus to the southwest suburbs of Chicago to see Robin's family again. I did this because I couldn't stay close to Robin because of all those court dates. I figured I ought to stay close to her family. Their support of me and what I was going through also helped give me strength.

Bill got me to the bus that took me down to the Loop to catch the Meta train to the Southside. I talked to the bus driver and he said he'd drop me close to the train station. However, he proceeded to drop me at the wrong station. As I walked down Randolph St., the wind penetrated my three layers of clothes with a thirty below wind chill. I hadn't been that cold since I was a child, playing hockey in outdoor rinks. The cold brought tears of pain to my eyes as it did when I was a child. Brutal.

Finally getting to my train, I started to warm up again as it lumbered to the Flossmoor Station. I think it took the entire forty-five minutes to warm up.

Jerry, Robin's father, picked me up and we went to his favorite Italian restaurant to have dinner with her brother David, his wife Jennifer, and the three boys. I always have fun with those boys as they jockey who will sit next to "Uncle John." I guess they think I'm a good uncle.

At last I got to sleep in a bed at Jerry's house. Oh, it was so nice to stretch out. On the way back to drop me off at the train, Jerry stopped at David's house to pick up a letter for me to give to the courts as to my character and ability to take care of my mother. It was one of many that healthcare professionals would write on my behalf. However, as I stated before, none of those letters or any of the evidence I'd collected would ever be seen by the judge's eyes. Too bad.

I was headed back to paradise thinking that I wouldn't have to return to Rockford until mid-May. It was quite a relief. On the flip side, however, I wouldn't be appointed Mom's guardian until then. That would leave us in limbo for a few more months.

Again, Arthur, Mom, and Snowy the dog picked me up at the Aspen Airport and even though it was mid-winter in the mountains, our cold is tropical by comparison to Chicago. Get out the Hawaiian shirts!

CHAPTER XVII

LIGHT AT THE END OF THE TUNNEL

One of the first things I did back in Aspen was to get in touch with the ACLU. I'd been trying to make a connection with them for months and finally did. My preconception of their work for human rights was that it was a David and Goliath sort of approach, but after I gave them Mom's information, they informed me I wasn't big enough for them and referred me to Equip for Equality in Rock Island, Illinois. And I always thought they fought for the little guy.

By this time I had sought help at many different agencies and learned that your second most valuable attribute, next to persistence, was patience. Both were needed to endure the endless waiting on the phone or games of phone tag that could take days. But patience and persistence are two of my best virtues.

So after many phone calls to Equip for Equality, I finally received a call back from their receptionist/intake person, Melinda. I guess they were tired of my squeaky wheel phone calls.

Melinda told me my mother's case sounded interesting and that she had passed it on to the head attorney in her office, Janet. Even though this wasn't a priority for me, I still thought it was a good move.

When I finally received the call back from Janet, she

explained that she couldn't help me with my case, but would look over it and that she had to create a new case for my mother. That was o.k. with me. At least maybe it would get the wheels rolling.

During our conversation, I mentioned Dad's attorney, Ms Rudy, and her behavior so far in court. Janet replied that her reputation precedes her and that she knew what I was up against in the 17th Judicial District courtroom. She only wished me luck, and said that what I was doing was admirable. I thanked her and assured her I'd keep in touch.

As I did more research on the computer, I stumbled on the circuit court website. After much fiddling around, I figured how to work the site. For me this would be a treasure trove of information that would make my life much easier.

The first thing I discovered was another court date that I hadn't been informed of. I wasn't about to be caught flat-footed again, so at the prompting of my girlfriend, I made arrangements to go back to Rockford for what I was told by Kim Timmerwilke was just another status hearing. But from my past experiences with the court, I thought I should be there because things are never as they appear, right?

With six weeks until court and tons to do, life went on and I was still trying to find a psychiatrist for Mom who would take Medicare, not an easy task in this Valley. I first had to find a new internist for Mom to get a referral to a psychiatrist.

All this took time, but we finally found Mom a new doctor. As I had done many times before with so many doctors, I explained Mom's situation, both mentally and physically, and how I got so lucky as to be doing what I was doing.

We got a referral to Dr. Wiley, the shrink, but it would be six weeks out till he could see her. We'd waited this long, so it was no problem. Mom was doing pretty well by then. In fact, she was getting more independent by the day.

During this time, Mom would go to lunch with Clem again, and to dinner with my friends. She'd always tag along. One dinner we had out with Papa Ouli and Peg, customers of mine, at Zheng, an Asian Pacific restaurant. This dinner really stuck out in my mind. Mom was thrilled and much more engaging at dinner than I'd seen her in years. It was then that I decided not to talk about her adjudication, or to try to analyze what she was saying and to just let her be herself.

There were other memorable dinners we'd have a friends' houses. One was at the Hankster's, with his wife Mary Pat and her brother Tony. The latter spent the evening serenading Mom with his guitar. How special!

It was one week until court and there was much to do, when I received a call from Bill in Rockford that would floor me. Bill told me to go online and look up one of the top news stories which was about a reward of twenty-five thousand dollars being offered for information on a "missing skull" from a 1948 unsolved double murder seventeen miles from Rockford. I didn't know if my father was involved, but he was eighteen years old at the time and living in the vicinity.

The murder was a double homicide that happened on Lover's Lane. One of the victims was a young sailor, and the other was a girl named Mary Jane Reed. This investigation was started by Mike Arians and after much persistence on his part, in 2005, they exhumed Mary Jane's body and through forensic pathology discovered that someone had switched her skull out and replaced it with another. I guess that made a possible three murders. Mary Jane was a petite woman and I thought the skull I held when I was nine years old could just as well be that of a small woman. I also remembered Mom's pictures I'd seen for years while growing up. Some were of old boyfriends and one happened to be a sailor from Rockford. This made the puzzle of the skull more interesting to me.

The article went on to state that whoever killed Mary Jane and her sailor boyfriend kept her skull as a souvenir. This article appeared not only in the local newspaper, but also in the <u>Chicago Tribune</u>. Strange, isn't it?

My next call was to Randy at the FBI to find out if he'd read the story. Randy said he hadn't, but would, and found my information very interesting and said he would look into the matter more carefully. Then I called Mike Arians in Oregon. He had his own theories, but found my story very fascinating and agreed to meet with me when I went back to Rockford.

This brought back to me a conversation Bill and I had about the mysterious cement patches in the basement of the family house that he lived in and the fact that my father kept a tub of lye in the basement. I also relayed this information to Randy at the FBI.

Continuing my research on my Mac on the big pharmaceutical companies, I hit pay dirt. Omnicare, a subsidiary of Johnson and Johnson, had been fined 2.8 billion dollars for kickbacks they gave to nursing homes in Illinois to use their psychotropic drugs on elders in nursing homes. Doctors were actually prescribing them off label, not for the approved use by the FDA, for people who didn't need them. In fact, they had used them on Mom at Alden Park Strathmoor and Floyd Schlossberg who owns Alden Healthcare was one of the companies investigated. How tragic.

This case went on to state that a doctor was guiding homeless people into this quagmire for profit and received six years in prison for his part. The puzzle I was doing was finally starting to fall into place. Medicare and Medicaid fraud, here we come. This was just one large regional area around Chicago where this was happening, but I believe it was only the tip of the iceberg. It's something we should all be furious about because it seems to be widespread and is costing the Medicare/Medicaid system billions, along with other illegal fraudulent schemes. We need to stand up and do battle; I can't do it alone.

Well, I was on the plane, heading back to Rockford and only God knew what lay ahead. I had a gut feeling that court would go well. I could only hope. My flight was normal, and I continued to write my book as I made the journey. Then I was on the bus and back to the hood. You know the scenario.

After my sleep in the chair with Lil' Dog, I was up and ready for court for hopefully my last pro se appearance.

Kim Timmerwilke met with me outside the courtroom and informed me I would receive my letters of guardianship of person, so I wouldn't have to appear in May. So what's second prize?

In the courtroom there was still a fear in the back of my mind that Ms Rudy might try to bring criminal charges of kidnapping against me. If that were to happen, I told Robin, my girlfriend, to call Connie Harvey, a friend of Mom's and mine, to bail me out or whatever. Connie has some connections at the state and federal levels and was my ace in the hole; another angel if you will.

Standing at the bench with Ms Rudy to my left and Kim Timmerwilke to my right, I informed the court as I'd done the four previous times that Mom's case and recovery were proceeding better than expected.

The court went ahead and made me guardian of person, but left my father as guardian of estate. Again I asked the court for an inventory of the house since I hadn't been in it in years. The only inventory I could remember was Mom's mother's piano, grandfather clock, and heirloom jewelry, and her Waterford crystal and clothes. I'd asked for those items twice before, and so far the courts just ignored my request. This time they said they'd look into it.

I asked Judge Fabiano about the bills since Ms Rudy asked the court to direct me to send any motions I filed directly to her and not my father, since this upset him. Even though my responsibilities were to notify all parties involved, Ms Rudy liked to bend the rules whenever she could, so I agreed to do this.

An odd thing happened just before this court date. My father, who had been in a nursing home for the previous five months, returned to his house the day before court. This was the house my mother should be living in. I think they thought I was going to attempt a power play to get the house back for Mom, but when I had requested this before, I was told by the court it was unfit for her to live in. Again, this made no sense because if it was unfit for my elderly mother, why wasn't it unfit for my elderly father? Follow the money.

Then, I again asked the court for Mom's back Social Security checks totaling sixteen hundred dollars, which we needed desperately so she could have her teeth fixed and not look like a toothless homeless person. Dental health is related to mental health. I had spent time with Dale, a Social Security agent in Glenwood Springs, who informed me that the money from Social Security follows the person. To knowingly withhold it is a direct violation of federal law, and a district court does not supersede federal law.

Ms Rudy again said that she'd look into it. She'd said

the same thing eight months before, so I didn't get my hopes up, since they had already violated Mom's civil rights across the board. I was realizing even more that the longer they drew this case out, the more money they could bill the estate until it was drained. That's the game they play. I'm sure this scenario takes place all across the country. I'm not alone, but I may be the first person to attempt to write a book about it. This needs to be stopped before it reaches epidemic proportions. Maybe it already has; I don't know.

To add insult to injury, Ms Rudy spoke again, pleading to the judge that I, the plaintiff, should be held responsible for her fees or a large part of them. It was then that she handed me a court filed motion of "rule to show cause" as to why I should be held responsible. I would think that, after their part in my mother's physical and psychological condition resulting in her being two pints short of blood, taking inappropriate medications, and having her civil rights violated, the court and its officers should be held accountable for their actions. Not in this court; not when you have such a corrupt system filled with probate sharks. I thought to myself that this just had to stop or change before the baby boomers reach this point.

Once again, Ms Rudy's only concern was not for Mom's well-being, but for how she and the guardian ad litem are going to be paid for the mess that they helped create.

After I thanked Judge Fabiano for her ruling on giving me guardian of person, I left her courtroom knowing full well I would have to come back to court in June to answer "rule to show cause." I met up with Kim Timmerwilke in the hallway outside the court, and Ms Rudy was also in the hall talking with her next clients. As I walked by, she looked up at me and gave me a hateful glare to which I just smiled, knowing that if she could, she'd probably object to my mere existence. At that point, I didn't think she had any idea what a thorn in her side I would become.

As I talked to Kim, I thanked her for not being so crass as to ask for her fees, even though Ms Rudy had asked for Kim's fees in her pleadings. I knew she understood that my mother needed teeth. Kim again informed me that she had no control over Ms Rudy's actions in court.

We bid our farewells, and I told Kim I'd keep in touch as guardian and see her in June for my final court date. After I got in the car and belted myself in, I finally had what was my only emotional breakdown. I started to cry, sucking air, so to say, in front of the courthouse. I didn't know what came over me. I think it was the fact that my mother, even though she was still adjudicated, wouldn't have to worry about the authorities in Colorado sending her back to Rockford to be thrown into a nursing home again and being medicated against her will. These fears would be unwarranted now that I was her guardian.

After stopping off at Bill's to freshen up after my breakdown, I kept my lawyer suit on and went off to search for platinum and gold records, medical records, that is. Once you're appointed guardian, you're privy to all your wards records. Since Ms Rudy made sure they were sealed in court, I was finally able to obtain them, which would make for an even more level playing field.

My first stop was at Swedish American Hospital. I went into the records department and the same woman who had given me Mom's evaluation report in May of 2009 was there. That had been when I had Mom's power of attorney for a brief time, which, by law, should not have been removed since I only had her best interest at heart. She checked out my letter of guardianship and said they'd have to send the records since it would be a fairly big file. I gave her my address and thanked them. I was then on my way to Park Strathmoor Nursing Home, and hoped they would be just as cooperative.

Knowing that the orders of protection stated I was to stay off their property, or they would be reinstated, I called ahead saying who I was and what I needed. I didn't, however, remind them of the orders of protection. They said it was no problem and I could come on out and fill out the necessary forms for the request.

I arrived at Alden Park Strathmoor and sat in the car for a moment and reflected on the last time I was there. At that time the police had pleaded ignorance of the law pertaining to powers of attorney, and the nursing home ignored them. I had to take my mother back into the nursing home crying that day in May. Then she was physically and sexually assaulted. How nice.

Finally I headed through the doors once again. I went up to the desk and was greeted by the receptionist who gave me the proper papers for my request. As I filled out the paper, the last question asked why I was making the request. The answer was multiple choice, and I checked the box that said for further medical evaluation.

As I waited for the administrator, I looked around and saw a few patients sitting around, numb, and waiting to die, while the others were locked down in the other corridors. It really felt like a prison. Poor souls.

Back to reality, the receptionist escorted me into the administrator's office. He stood, gave me a firm handshake, and asked what he could do for me. I replied that I needed Mom's records of her stay at their institution for her further medical care.

The administrator looked down at my request form,

flipped through a few pages, and then looked straight at me and said, "Is this for the lawsuit?" To which I quickly assured him it was not. Not at this time. It was for what I had stated. He said he'd look into the request and get back to me. He went further and said he didn't think it would be a problem.

As I walked back to the car, I thought it was a pretty pointed question he asked about the lawsuit since I'd never brought it up to anybody. It was pretty much at the bottom of my list of things to do.

My final stop before a little R & R was the police department. Through the Freedom of Information Act, I could get all the police reports pertaining to my actions in May of 2009 at Park Strathmoor and the record of Mom's subsequent escape from Rockford four months later. The counter women were very helpful, saying they would have to send them. But they said they couldn't find the report on the incident at Park Strathmoor when I tried to remove Mom in May, only to be greeted by seven men in blue with guns. Surely they must have filed a report. I paid a nominal fee, thanked them, and left.

That night, when Bill, his youngest son Matt, and I were at dinner, I filled Bill in on court and obtaining the medical and police records. I then asked him if he'd like to go with me to see Mike Arians at the Road House Cafe in Oregon, Illinois, to talk with him about the reward for the skull and give him the information I had on the one I held in my hand so along ago. I told Bill we could make a day of it and to bring Matt along for the ride, thinking it would be good fun. He accepted, and then I was off to my Lazy Boy chair with Lil' Dog for a good night's sleep. Long Day.

I woke up to a cool spring day, put on blue jeans and a ball cap and was off to Oregon for a nice Sunday drive with Bill and his son for a family day. As we meandered down

IL 2 winding along the river, I worked as tour guide for Matt. I pointed out Stronghold Castle and the enormous statue of Chief Blackhawk overlooking the river, a place I'd played around when we'd go camping in my youth. I finally showed him Lover's Lane, where Mary Jane Reed and her sailor boyfriend from Rockford had been brutally murdered in 1948. How eerie.

When we arrived at the Road House, Matt stayed in the car and Bill and I went in. It was a western looking building on a busy intersection, like out of a movie. As I looked upstairs to a window, I noticed a blond manikin dressed up in a period costume from the forties. I pointed it out to Bill and we agreed it creeped us both out.

At the bar, we asked if Mike was in. They told us they'd get him and at that point I ordered a beer. I then realized that sitting across from me was a beautiful brunette manikin posed as if she were alive. I was hoping it wouldn't get any creepier. I guess I've seen too many horror flicks.

Mike arrived and invited Bill and me out to his motor home to talk, and as we followed him, I was praying that there weren't any more of those creepy manikins. As we entered, I looked around, and there weren't. Thank God.

Mike filled me in on everything in the case of Mary Jane Reed and was adamant about it. After half an hour or so, I started to tell him my story and the timeline. This must have been too much for Bill to handle, because he excused himself and said he'd wait in the car.

After finishing my story and telling Mike that I had also contacted the FBI, I asked how the food was in his restaurant and he invited us to stay and even picked up the bill.

As we ate, I looked around and could tell we were in

rural America from the clientele and the fact that Oregon is a small town with very little crime not far from Rockford. The food was good as was the conversation about the plastic girls in the windows and bar.

Then it was back on the road to the hood and a good night's sleep. I would make my escape back home the next day. I was outta there.

CHAPTER XVIII

PAUL'S LAST STAND?

While en route back to Aspen, I received a call on my short layover in Denver. It was Pam, my friend Paul Soldner's caregiver. She was pretty frantic, saying that Paul was on his deathbed and wanted to see me. I couldn't refuse; this was for Paul, and for me. Since I had some time at the airport, I used up all my miles and got a free ticket to California. I'd only be home three days with Mom before leaving to see Paul. I was so tired of jet setting, especially when there was so little fun involved.

Everything was a-okay at home at the metal cabin. Then it was off to California to see Paul, and the best thing was I got to see my princess, even if it was only for a few days. It had been quite a transition from seeing my girl once a month to twice a year; it wasn't easy. But she understood and we managed.

I was back in California and warm again. Robin and I headed for dinner. She had made reservations, which was a good idea since my princess is not very familiar with the kitchen. After a superb meal at The Godfather's, it was home to sleep in a California king-size bed.

The next morning, after I made breakfast for my girl, Alan, a friend of mine came to pick me up. He is the other half of Alan-and-Suzi and they are two of only a handful of my straight friends out there. Alan had met Paul before and didn't mind taking me up to Claremont, near L.A., to see him.

As we drove, I didn't know what to expect, so I called Pam on the way. She told me Paul was feeling better, making somewhat of a comeback, and having a good day.

We arrived about noon. Paul was up and around, moving slowly, but was still with us in every sense of the word. After some chit-chat and small talk, we had lunch. After an hour and a half, Paul was tired, so I was back in the car driving to San Diego to relax and write for a couple of days.

As I always do when I'm in San Diego, I did the house chores on Robin's honey-do list that she can't handle herself. Then I spent some time with my gay boys and Robin, and then I was off to the airport and back to Aspen.

On the way to the airport in San Diego, I received a call from Arthur, my roommate, telling me that Mom had gone over the fence, not the fence some people go over in marriage, but the real six-foot fence in front of my place. He said she was ok, but angrier than a swarm of hornets. She was at my neighbor Laney's house and didn't want to come home until I got there. All I could think was this was going to be interesting.

Robin dropped me off at the airport, kissed me goodbye, and said, "I hope I'll see you sooner rather than later this time." She told me to hang in there. She has MS and could see by the way I was caring for Mom that I'd be a perfect caregiver for her if that day ever came.

Heading east back to Aspen, I arrived early. It was nice when your flights are on time. Arthur picked me up at the airport, but without Mom for the first time. She must be really pissed off.

Arthur filled me in on the way home. Apparently he over-slept and Mom wanted to go for a walk. The gate on the fence was locked and she didn't want to wake him, so she went to the shed, grabbed an eight foot ladder, leaned it against the fence and climbed over, only to end up in the bed of my Ford pick-up truck. It must've been quite a sight! This supposedly frail old lady, who, nine months before, could hardly walk from the abuse she received back in Rockford, was now crawling over fences. It was hard to believe.

After she got in the bed of the truck, one of my Hispanic neighbors came to her rescue and helped Mom out of the truck. With the language barrier, this must have been pretty funny.

Before Mom completed her escape, Arthur appeared and told Mom to go back in the house, and as you can imagine, this pissed her off even more. After what Arthur called a heated argument, Mom went for her walk. After she returned, she went to Laney's next door, and she told Arthur she wouldn't come home until I returned.

Mom was at the gate with Laney when we pulled up; then she and Arthur started their heated debate and shouted back and forth all the way into the kitchen. Mom was so mad that she was frothing at the mouth. When she started yelling at Arthur, calling him "a horse's ass," I think it was only the third time I would yell at Mom. I'd had enough of her selfishness and called her an "ungrateful fucking bitch." She reeled back from Arthur, looked at me and said, "You, you, you and your one inch dick."

I immediately started to laugh and responded right away with, "It's only an inch when I fold it in half; you must have been thinking about Dad."

With that, Mom hustled off to her bedroom, and the next day she apologized to Arthur. He returned it as well. No blood, no foul.

What happened next almost took me to the point of no return. Mom gets an unlucky break.

CHAPTER XIX
MOM GETS A BREAK

Things went smoothly for the next couple of weeks after my return from California, but that would all change on April 12, 2010. That date would live on in my mind in infamy.

It was a beautiful spring day as Mom and I went into town so I could make a couple of house calls. Mom stayed in the car during my first one, reading magazines in the Colorado sun. While I was at my dental hygienist Kelly Keefe's house, however, halfway through her hair appointment, the sun started to set. I decided to bring Mom in the house so she could get warm and also listen to Kelly's son, Lincoln, practice his Bach on the piano.

Mom got up from her chair in the living room and headed to the den to listen to young Lincoln practice. Before Kelly or I could make a move, Mom, who couldn't see the seven-inch step down to the den, fell, causing an extremely loud "thump," followed by screaming, "I broke my hip!" This hit me like a ton of bricks because like most people I've known who have broken their hips or who I've read about in my research, this could be the beginning of the end for her.

Kelly and I were at her side immediately, and she repeated that she thought she had broken her hip. As we tried to move her, she went on to say, "Just let me lay here for a minute." Then, after she calmed down and we had checked her hip, Mom looked over to Lincoln who was still sitting at the piano, and said, "Go ahead and finish playing. I was enjoying that so much." Kelly and I looked at each other in disbelief, and I thought, "This is one tough woman."

After Lincoln finished playing, the three of us got Mom to her feet. She said she couldn't put much pressure on them, but didn't want to go to the hospital because she wasn't sure it was broken.

It took us about ten minutes to load Mom in the car. I said goodbye to Kelly and her son and told her I'd keep her updated, and we headed down valley.

It took about fifteen minutes to get Mom into the house. I suspected that her hip was truly broken, but she said she just wanted to lie down for a while. So I got her to bed and for the next hour or so I checked on her every fifteen minutes.

When the pain finally got the best of her, I dialed "911" to bring in the troops, so we wouldn't have to carry her to the car. I'd just leave it to the professionals. From that moment on, things became very surreal.

When the Basalt Fire and Rescue arrived, I told Mom the Chippendale boys were there to transport her to the hospital. I guess we got our first male angels during this saga.

After they put her on a backboard and carried her through the house, I could tell by the moans and groans that her hip was surely broken. As they loaded Mom into the ambulance, I told them to take her down valley to the hospital in Glenwood Springs and thanked them profusely. They were so professional for a volunteer department.

Shortly thereafter, I was in the car on my way to the

hospital. It was 11:00 p.m. When I arrived, I knew it was going to be a long night.

They had already given Mom a pain killer when I arrived, so that look of agony had left her face. After I filled out the proper paperwork, it was off to the x-ray department. When the doctor came in, he told us that she'd broken the hip and they'd be admitting her that night.

Luckily for us, Valley View Hospital looks, and is run like, a five-star resort, and there was actually a fold-down sofa bed in Mom's room. Because of her fear of institutions, I told her I'd stay the night.

The next day, I was able to make some house calls to keep some cash flow going. I knew that this was going to be a lean week, and I was already strapped for cash.

Assuming that all Mom's insurances were in place, I proceeded to meet with her medical team. The first was the orthopedic surgeon, Dr. St. John's, physician's assistant. She explained to me the procedure for hip surgery. The other option, doing nothing, would have meant nursing home placement and resulted in Mom's being bedridden for the rest of her life. We scratched that.

My main concern, though, was the anesthesiologist. I was worried about how Mom would fare due to her inability to absorb medication because of her gastric by-pass surgery. Another concern was that any senior going through major surgery risked the after effects of medical delirium. With the medical knowledge of present day, there could be issues. The doctors don't know how much is caused by the injury, the medication, or anesthesia. They just don't know.

As our population gets older, I see this becoming an even greater problem. Medical delirium can last from a few hours to a few days. It can also become permanent and accelerate dementia, Alzheimer's, and memory loss. It can produce agitation and other mood behaviors causing the doctor to prescribe psychotropic or anti-psychotic drugs, which you've seen as you've followed my story, can be a slippery slope. This was a situation which needed to be addressed sooner, rather than later, as I would find out on my journey with Mom.

The third day at the hospital, it was all systems go for surgery. I first met with Dr. McDerrmont and expressed my concerns. Dr. McDerrmont was a petite, pretty, girl. And young. It's funny, how as we get older, our doctors start looking like our children. It just doesn't seem right. However, she was very professional as we spoke, even though we decided on general anesthesia, she assured me she would barely take Mom under. I thanked her and told her she was the most important doctor in the room for Mom.

Then I met with the surgeon, Dr. St. John. I'd heard the name for years. Living in a mountain ski town, you get to know the name of the orthopedists because it's a dangerous place. Instead of injuries caused by guns and violence, we have lots of broken bones and torn ligaments. And sometimes death, when the trees don't get out of your way. Dr. St. John is also much younger than his reputation implies.

Upon meeting Dr. St. John, I told him I'd already talked to the most important doctor who would be in the operating room that day, Dr. McDerrmont. He chuckled, and then proceeded to explain the procedure he'd be performing.

With that done, everything was set for surgery. Mom wasn't the least bit scared, so they wheeled her into the operating room.

I waited until after surgery to make sure everything was a-ok and that Mom was back in her room. Then I took off for Aspen to do more customers' hair. For the next five days, this same scenario would take place. I slept on the sofa bed in Mom's room, then made the eighty-mile round trip to work, chasing the dollar.

Something wasn't right. Mom was agitated and resentful of being in the hospital, and in some state of medical delirium, but I just didn't know how bad it was. I knew they medicated her for agitation and would only find out much later how much this fueled the fire.

The nice thing, besides the fact that they run the hospital like a five-star resort, is that they have volunteer musicians come into your room and play anything from country to classical music. That really gave Mom a boost, as it did the other patients. This is something I feel should be integrated into all our healthcare institutions, including nursing homes. I believe that in those regimented, sterile environments, the comfort music provides fosters the full recovery of the patients.

Mom was then transferred to Heritage Nursing Home to rehabilitate before I could take her home. This was the same facility I'd looked into for future placement for Mom. I'd even had a good working relationship with the admissions director, Susan Reed, who had been ever so helpful when Mom first arrived in August of 2009. Mom and I had visited the facility many times when my good friend Dr. Dan was there recuperating after hip replacement.

Mom was, however, pretty upset about being in an institution again, and was often agitated toward the staff. She had a lot of distrust after her experiences in Rockford. Can you blame her?

Although this facility wasn't perfect, it could teach the Illinois facilities a lot about giving people dignity and respect. I'd watch how every employee, from the physical therapist to the administrator, would don different hats as they were needed to help in each person's care. On many of my twenty visits in twenty-one days, I'd have lunch with Mom and her new boyfriend and watch all the employees, including the administrator, serve coffee and help feed their patients. It always seemed to be a group effort. Well done.

The third week into Mom's rehab, I got a call from Susan. She informed me that after twenty-one days, Mom would have to be released because there was no supplement to her Medicare. Apparently, under my father's and his attorney Rudy's watch, her insurance expired, and they didn't notify the court or me. Here the very people who had fought me for the right to take care of Mom had shown their ineptness again. They screwed it up.

So there I was, with no money from Mom's owed Social Security that Ms Rudy and my father were withholding. I was forced to take Mom home and try to rehabilitate her myself. And as you can tell, I'm always up for a challenge...not.

I got the house ready for Mom's return, making sure there were no obstacles for her to trip over. Her walker was set up in the bathroom so it was handicap-friendly, shower and all. And then I went to retrieve her.

Mom's happy about getting out, even though she doesn't get around that well. I thought a couple more weeks of rehab would have helped, but there we were, on our own to fend for ourselves again. I was back to cooking four meals a day, helping her bathe, and trying to work. I never thought I would have to be a mom myself.

Then I saw that mom's mental state wasn't right and called her former internist, asking for a referral to a psychiatrist. I was told that for insurance reasons, they wouldn't do this, and they referred me to another doctor down valley in Glenwood.

I don't recall his name, but the doctor was a good ol' Texas boy about my age. He looked over Mom, checked out her meds, prescribed more Vicodin for pain, and gave me a referral to Dr. Wiley, a psychiatrist. However, that appointment would be another two weeks out. So with Mom's mental state not improving, I decided to take her on a farewell tour back to Rockford to see her children and grand children. It would be a long, but, I hoped pleasant, drive.

The day we were to leave, I ran and got six spliffs for the road; unlike a lot of people, they keep me hyper and alert. Go figure. Then I retrieved my mail and found a letter from Ms Rudy's office. I sat in the Cougar as I opened it, but there was no message from her. There was just a bill from Bruce Person's office that I was instructed to mail her. Apparently Ms Rudy and I weren't in the same courtroom, or she had total disregard for what the judge said. I think it's the latter. I guess she thought she ran the show her way. Oh well, I just didn't get it. So it was off to Rockford, and a court date I could only hope would go my way.

CHAPTER XX
FAREWELL TOUR

I loaded up the Cougar with a cooler full of food and drinks and got Mom into the car for the 24 hours to Rockford. That's about how long the drive is, and since I had so little money and even less time, I knew that in the next seven days I'd drive over 3,000 miles. And most of it would be non-stop. Whoa.

Having done this drive many times during my thirty years in Aspen, I was pretty prepared. However, I hadn't driven those distances since I was young, and I wasn't sure that as a middle-aged man I'd have the same stamina.

So we were off on our journey, our farewell tour. I was hoping it wouldn't be Mom's last, but she wasn't doing very well mentally or physically, so I just didn't know.

It was 1:00 p.m. on the Wednesday before Memorial Day when I pulled the car onto Highway 82 toward Glenwood Springs. I expected to have a lot of traffic during the day, but would definitely make up the time with my overnight driving. And I had my spliffs to keep me awake.

I didn't have to be in court until Monday, so we had plenty of time. Mom settled back into her bucket seat and I became a driving fool.

About an hour and a half out, I realized I'd forgotten my court summons for jury duty in Aspen. The court date was the same as the one in Rockford. The jury summons was for Charlie Sheen's trial for domestic assault on his wife at Christmas when he held a knife to her throat. It must be that "tiger blood." So I called a friend of mine who's a sheriff, and he told me that the courts give you one no-show before they charge you with contempt. That was a relief, so I was on my way.

The drive was pretty uneventful. Mom was a little scared, going back to Rockford, and told me she was afraid they'd put her back in that awful nursing home and that she'd get beat up again. I assured her that I was now in charge of her and I wouldn't let that happen in a million years. I hoped that would give her some comfort, but wasn't sure.

As we drove, we listened to Mom's favorite country singer, Toby Keith, over and over, the whole way home. I liked the CD, and learned to sing every song on the trip, but it was a little much. It was soothing for her, though.

I also made a little game every hundred miles or so of taking a toke off a joint to stay awake. Then every three hours, we'd stop to stretch and pee or whatever. I would usually put Mom in the wheelchair and roll her up to the bathroom. Sometimes, though, she'd take so long that I'd ask another female traveling on the Interstate to check on her in the bathroom. Since I was in the heartland of the country, people were ever so helpful.

We arrived in Rockford at Bill's barber shop about 3:00 p.m. on Thursday. Mom and I were really tired, even though she'd slept most of the way. This was the first time Bill and his children Mark, Goobs, and Matt had seen Mom since the day of her escape. There were many hugs and a lot of tears and laughter after so much pain. It made the whole drive worth it. Even though Mom wasn't in the condition she'd been in during the previous nine months, there was still so much happiness and love.

Bill had the house set up for Mom and me, a bedroom in the living room for her, and my Lazy Boy and Lil' Dog for me. Mom was so happy to be with her children, but she was thrilled off the charts to have her Lil' Dog, Pierre.

We were so exhausted that we both got a good night's sleep. With Mom's delirium, that was rare. So with much to do the next day, we were up, showered, dressed, and out the door.

I stopped to see a friend of mine, Mikey, and he told me that Diane, a childhood friend, was trying to get in touch with me. It was a good thing, because when I got hold of Di, she offered me her spare bedroom, which I gladly accepted. Bill assured me that he was up to the task of watching Mom at night, so I finally got a bed. Yeah.

About 4:00 Friday afternoon, I received a rather frantic call from Kim Timmerwilke telling me that court on Monday had been cancelled. The reason was Ms Rudy hadn't had enough time to go over my answers to "rule to show cause." That was funny, since I had it filed in time. I didn't know what the problem could be since my answers were fairly simple. Since I'm not a lawyer, they weren't full of legalese. Kim went on to say that she hoped I hadn't left yet and that it wouldn't be an inconvenience for me.

I told her not at all, that I'd just driven 1,100 miles with my mother, why should I be upset? This was only the second time they'd cancelled or moved a court date without informing me in a fair and timely manner. Kim apologized to me, but I told her not to worry; it wasn't her fault. I said that everything was fine and she shouldn't be apologizing for Ms Rudy's tactics. Before hanging up, I said I'd see her in court in July.

Friday night, my childhood friend Diane had a party at her house. We first met back in junior high school. We became friends and I referred to her as my little sister. Di invited Bill, Mom, and me to the party. We accepted; however, I told her about Mom's condition. Before her hip break, Mom would have one glass of wine a week, but because of her precarious mental health, I asked Di not to offer her anything to drink. She said she'd help watch that.

The party was great. I saw people I hadn't seen since high school, mostly women. There were Sharon and Karen and Gay and a few others I didn't remember.

About an hour into the party, as I was grilling steaks, someone poured Mom a small glass of wine. Oops. It didn't go so well. She got dizzy and sleepy and had to lie on Diane's fainting couch. While we ate, she was soon fast asleep as the party continued around her.

That shortened the party for Bill and me, and I helped Bill get Mom in the car and back to the hood house. After Mom was settled in at Bill's, I headed back to Di's and partied a little longer, getting reacquainted with old friends. Then it was off to sleep in a bed alone where I could stretch out all six feet four inches of me. Nice sleep over, eh?

I was up early on Saturday, and Di made a delicious breakfast. After a little more small talk, I was on my way to the southwest burbs to see Robin's sister–in–law Jennifer's mother Liz who was in a nursing home rehab facility after having a brain tumor removed.

As I drove the Cougar down Interstate 90, I had another stop on the way in Rolling Meadows because I had something for Joey. She's Roxy's sister from Aspen, and Roxy had given me clothes for her. I'd known Joey, or Jo Ann, for 25 years. She's developmentally disabled and had been institutionalized since she was very young.

Arriving at the one-level facility, I went to the secured door, and after buzzing the buzzer, I was let in. I checked in at the nurse's station and was helped by a black male nurse from Ethiopia. I asked for Joey and he flipped on his computer and told me she could be either in the shower or in her room within a matter of seconds.

Again the technology was great, available, and inexpensive. He simply turned on the computer, and he could see all the common areas where the residents were. This eliminated the stress of running around looking for them. This should become mandatory in all facilities, nursing homes, etc. across the country. Not only would this free up employees for more important tasks, it would also curb elopement where countless elders and such die every year because of lack of security like this and recklessness.

They determined that Joey was in her room and went to bring her to me. I introduced myself to her and let her know I had gifts from Roxy. She got very excited and kept saying, "Where's Fobbi?" I looked around at the residents; some of them were deformed, blind, or deaf, but functional and happy. This was a facility that did things right, so I knew it was possible.

For the next hour I was with Joey, she held the sweaters and blouses up to her chin and across her chest to see how they would look. This in itself made up for what I thought was a wasted drive back to Illinois.

When I got ready to leave, Joey wanted to come with me and kept saying, "Me go to McDonald with you." I told Joey I had to get permission from Roxy, and that I'd be back and take her there in the fall.

After a few pictures were taken of us and many hugs shared, I was on my way to see Liz. I made it to the Southside in record time, since I had to be back in Rockford for dinner.

Meeting up with Jen and David, we drove to the nursing home. This place happened to be first class. It had new equipment and was nicely decorated and very clean. Liz was in good spirits when I first greeted her. She had a black woman who was a former school teacher as her roommate. I'm not sure what she was there for; however, Liz was rehabbing from the removal of a non-malignant brain tumor. At lunchtime, one of the staff brought in lunch. Liz got a little agitated and didn't want to eat because she had company. Robin's brother David, a doctor, convinced her she had to eat to help with her recovery.

David helped by cutting up her food as his wife Jennifer and I watched. After about fifteen minutes, we noticed that the black woman was struggling to eat her meal. After twenty minutes, I saw David's doctor instincts kick in, and he took it upon himself to go over to this woman and sit on the edge of the bed and start to feed her. I'd never seen David as a doctor. There he was as a visitor, doing someone else's job, and what great bedside manners he had. I was impressed.

When someone finally arrived, David took them aside in the hallway and gave them a piece of his mind about their level of care. He wasn't happy. Here again I was in a nursing home that looked first class, but wasn't. I was starting to believe that they were all about maximum profit and minimum care.

After lunch, I gave Liz hugs and kisses and said that I'd see her at Thanksgiving. We got in the car and headed to Aurelio's to meet Robin's father and the boys, Andy, Ben, and Sam, for pizza.

On the way there, I brought up the incident at the

nursing home to David. He stated that he was pretty disgusted with what he saw, and further said that that's why he didn't work for their company that also owns a hospital. It's pretty amazing that these health institutions get away with such low levels of care. Our only hope for the future is to rise up and stop this bullshit.

On a lighter note, lunch with the boys and Robin's father Jerry is always good fun. I'd only been dating his daughter for 14 years and he still liked to bust my chops as if I were still green. But it was all in good fun and great training for the boys in this genre of life skills.

The pizza was gone and so was I, heading back to the hood. I arrived just in time for dinner, steaks on the grill, beer, the works. No wonder I was gaining weight.

Mom was doing ok and seemed pretty happy, but a little confused about being back in Rockford. Like I said earlier, I wished I could have brought her back in the condition she was in before she broke her hip. I didn't have to, nor would I have taken Mom to court. This would have given them the "I told you so" defense. I wouldn't let them know of her mental condition, just her physical state. I knew that if court was delayed long enough, Mom would get older and that maybe, just maybe, something would happen to her just like it had, and they'd have a self-fulfilling prophecy. That's why when you're dealing with elders in a court situation, things should be expedited, not delayed, because it does that person and their family a great disservice.

We finished dinner, and then I helped Bill get Mom ready for bed. As we covered her up, Lil' Dog jumped under the covers. He remembered Mom well, as she remembered him, since he was her dog before she was put in the nursing home. Soon they were fast asleep, and I was off to Di's house to sleep as well.

It was Memorial Day and I woke up, got ready, and had breakfast with Di. Then I was off to pick up Bill and Mom and head to the cemetery to visit and clean up my brother Marc's and Mom's parents' graves. We stopped at Farm and Fleet for some tools for the job at hand.

We found the gravesite and I asked Bill to drive over to it since it was a long way from the road. The grave plaques are all recessed, so it shouldn't be a problem. But Bill refused, saying he'd have to drive over graves.

So we unloaded Mom and her walker and made our way across the graves. At some point, I told Bill he was walking on graves and he replied, "I'm nuts over every one." This brought a burst of laughter from Mom and me. I guess she still had a sense of humor.

We cleaned up the graves, and for some odd reason fire ants were swarming on Marc's grave. I remarked, "He wasn't that sweet."

Then we asked Mom if she'd like to talk to her parents, and she said, "I'll be doing that soon enough." After finishing, we headed back to the house, going through what was left of downtown Rockford.

Mom pointed out different points of interest and things she remembered from her childhood. She told us what used to be in each building. Her memories seemed all right, but her medical delirium was driving us both crazy.

At Bill's house, Mom settled in for a nap with Lil' Dog, so I was off to visit my friend Doak's mother, Do Ann. She was in her nineties and not doing so well, but she lived at home by herself and was adamant about not letting the visiting nurses' association in to check on her. That must be common knowledge passed down by other seniors. They knew that if the nurse came and didn't like what she saw, you were off to the nursing home against your will. I guess the older, the wiser.

Do Ann, even though she was slowed by age, still had that special sparkle in her blue eyes I remembered. We sat a spell and talked about the old days when I used to be a Shrine clown in the circus with her husband Lloyd, and how I used to clown at the Special Olympics. She talked further about her children and grand children, telling about how often she got to see them and how helpful they were in keeping her in her home. I was fairly envious; this was how it should have been for Mom. But I was afraid Ms Rudy and her court only fractured a family. I'd be seeing Ms Rudy the next day.

Saying goodbye to Do Ann was difficult for me because I didn't know if I would see her again on this side.

After our goodbyes, I went back to check up on Mom and then drove over to Di's to get ready for a night out on the town with the girls.

I rode with Janice, and Di and Karen rode together, and we headed to Maria's Italian Restaurant. As always, the food was fab, and so was the company, just me and the girls.

After dinner we all decided to go out dancing. I had a good martini buzz going, so even with a sore hip, I was game. We ended up at The Office, a gay bar that my gay nephew, Goobs, frequented. I must've been really buzzed because by the end of the evening I'd be dancing on a pedestal wearing a lampshade. Oh so much fun! But since we were older, we didn't close the bar. I slipped back to Di's, since I had court kind of early the next morning.

On awakening the next day, my head felt like a big

tomato, so I had a little coffee and breakfast to shake the cobwebs from my head. I dressed in my suit and went off to court.

On the way downtown, I received a call from Kim Timmerwilke telling me that even though the judge had cancelled the June first court date, she agreed to see me on June second, since I'd driven so far. Hearing that, I headed back to Di's, got out of my suit, then drove over to Bill's to help my youngest nephew take care of Mom.

Mom hadn't had a shower in two days, so I asked Matt to help me. Since he was only fifteen, I explained to him how I'd helped Grandpa Howard give Gram a bath. I told him jokingly not to look. Mom would take her towel off after she was behind the shower curtain, and Matt would help me by handing me shampoo, conditioner, and whatever else I needed to get the job done.

When we were done, Matt gave Grandma a towel behind the shower curtain and then we helped her out. As we left the bathroom, I looked at Matt and said, "You became a man today, and what you've just helped do should stay with you the rest of your life." Just as it did with me. He smiled.

We spent the rest of the day with Mom, doing her hair, watching TV, eating, and waiting for Bill to come home. All in all, it was a good day. When Bill got home, and Mom was settled in, I was off to Di's to eat dinner with her and Karen.

It was a quiet night, so after dinner and some time in the hot tub, I was soon fast asleep, and would be in much better condition for court the next day.

After breakfast the next morning, I talked with Ms Timmerwilke again, and she stated that she wouldn't be in court. She added that most likely Ms Rudy wouldn't be there either, so I would probably be able to present my evidence without Ms Rudy's objections.

Well, I was finally in court with no Kim and no Ms Rudy. As I sat there pondering what I was about to say, Ms Rudy swaggered in. We'd see how this goes. We both approached the bench, and as always, I informed Judge Fabiano about Mom's condition and care. Then I started to tell her how, acting as Mom's guardian, my father had messed up her health insurance and what I did to correct this. Ms Rudy, as she had always done, turned up her lip and objected to what I was saying. At that point, I didn't know, but I was pretty sure she would object to my mere existence. The judge let me finish, but as to the rest of my case, I'd have to wait until all the officers of the court, meaning Kim Timmerwilke, were there. I'd have to wait till the July hearing in three weeks.

Before being excused, I asked the judge about the bill's again, and told her, over the objections of Ms Rudy, that they sent the last bill back to me. Ms Rudy tried to explain, but she made no sense whatsoever. Then Judge Fabiano directed me to continue to have them sent directly to Ms Sharon Rudy. I felt like it was a hollow victory for me, but at least they had to pay the bills.

Outa court, outa there. Back at Bill's hood house, I loaded Mom up for our last stop at Bill's daughter, Danielle's, in the upper peninsula of Michigan. It was an easy seven hour drive, so I took a toke and we were off.

As I drove north on Interstate 90, we approached Madison, Wisconsin, and on the horizon was the darkest thunderhead I'd seen in years. Not wanting to drive through a tornado or two, I called Danielle and asked her to check the weather forecast. About the time she told me it was ok after Madison, all hell broke loose and that thunderhead let go of all its glaring lightning. It rained so hard I had to pull over on the shoulder and hit the four-way flasher and pray that we didn't let hit by another vehicle bearing down from the rear or by a tornado. For one of the few times in my life, I was scared to death. Mom seemed to be lackadaisical; I'm not sure that in her condition she understood the imminent danger we were in.

After what seemed like an eternity, about fifteen minutes, the storm lightened up. As the southbound cars passed slowly by, there were lots of broken or missing windshields. I guess I dodged a bullet.

So we drove on, arriving at Danielle and Matt's, her second husband. I hadn't seen them since their wedding in Las Vegas. Danielle lost her first husband in Iraq, who was fighting for the very freedoms my mother was denied. His name was Gary Harper, Jr. He was a staff sergeant doing recognizance work when he was shot. A couple of years later, his best friend Matt, who was with him in Iraq, fell in love with and married Gary's widow, Danielle. He took on her three children, and they now had two of their own.

Danielle was ecstatic to see her Grandma, even though our visit would last less than twelve hours. Mom wasn't doing so hot and becoming increasingly more agitated. So after giving Danielle some of her artwork, taking pictures with her grandkids and great grandkids, and a reluctant shower in the morning I had one more stop at the bank. Danielle had said she could cash a check for me before I left Rockford, but when we got there, she didn't have enough funds in the bank. With little choice, because I would need gas money, I headed back to Rockford. This would put about five hours more on a twenty-four hour trip. That's life.

I swooped down to Rockford for a whistle stop at Bill's shop. He handed me two hundred dollars and I was on my way.

Mom slept most of that night. Except for our bathroom breaks, she was quiet. We finally stopped for food in Nebraska at an all-night McDonald's, and after eating, she got very defiant and didn't want to go with me. A good thing was that a couple of state police were eating, and I told Mom her only other choice would be to go with them. I was out of options. Mom must have been cognitive enough to remember her last run-in with the law because she reluctantly got into the car for the rest of the journey.

It wasn't until we were in Vail that things went from bad to worse. She reached over, trying to hold my hand like I was my father. Instinctively, I pulled my hand away; then she got mad, saying how she'd given me children, and how could I treat her like that, and that she'd always loved me. This spooked me out, but in hindsight, I should've played along.

By the time we arrived at the house, she refused to go in. After a lot of coaxing, I got Mom to the front door, and as were about to enter, she placed a hand on either side of the door jam and pushed back on me so hard she knocked my sunglasses off and accidentally stepped on them. As they shattered on the porch, she started screaming at the top of her lungs, "Help! He's beating me!"

CHAPTER XXI

HELP! HE'S BEATING ME!

With Mom still pushing back against me as I stood in the broken glass, the neighbors who could hear her screams looked over at us. I scooped Mom up underneath her arms and carried her into the house. I sat her down on a dining room chair, and as fast as she had started to yell, she was all of a sudden quiet and emotionless. I knew I had to do something quickly, so I called my friend Jackie and explained what had just happened. I told her I was tired from my 1,800 mile, almost nonstop, drive and that I needed help fast.

Jackie was fast, and after only twenty minutes showed up at the trailer with her husband, Dan, in tow. She had come down because Mom had refused to get back in the car with me. I think she thought I was Dad, I don't know. While we were talking outside, Mom suddenly became more compliant and agreed to ride with me to the hospital, but only if they followed. Mom had developed a relationship with Dan and Jackie, so this made it much easier.

At the ER, Jackie and Dan helped me get Mom to the doors, and then waited outside while I checked her in. This done, I went back outside, thanked them, and said, "I can take over from here," and that I'd keep them informed.

Mom perked up at the hospital; me, not so much. I was tired from the long drive. The nurses came in after a while and took her vitals and some blood, and then asked me to explain why we were there. I explained the best I could and then waited for the doctor. It was late when he got around to us, and after listening to me and examining Mom, he said there was not much he could do. He had one of the nurses call a psychiatrist and he called back in about five minutes. The doctor and I both spoke to him and he said he couldn't accept Medicare because he had almost been charged with fraud before, but he would write a prescription for Xanax to keep her calm. She was to take one every four hours for agitation. They gave me a script and a few samples to hold us over till I could get the prescription the next day. Finally we were able to go home and I hoped this would work until we could see Dr. Wiley when he got back from vacation.

Mom seemed better the next day. Her hip was still sore, so she was now taking a Xanax and a Vicodin every four to eight hours. It kept her calm, but did nothing to help her mental state.

This went on for a couple of days. I did the best I could; however, she was in no shape to go on house calls with me. Since I couldn't make house calls, I missed a few clients.

The third morning after the ER visit, Mom woke up agitated, primarily because she wasn't sleeping through the night, and she refused to take a shower. This was a problem, but finally I coaxed her in.

She got herself dressed and her make-up on, but then started to complain that her stomach hurt. I had to cancel my day and it was back to the ER Instead of Aspen Valley Hospital, though, I turned right on Highway 82 and headed to Glenwood Springs to Valley View Hospital. I was hoping for a better diagnosis there. On the way, I called Mom's favorite nephew, Steve, and asked him to meet us there because Mom was belligerent and he could always calm her down.

Steve met us in the waiting room of the ER Mom and I hadn't checked in because she refused. But after forty-five minutes, Steve and I talked her into going in. She was just plain nasty to all the female nurses and aides and said that she couldn't pee for the specimen. This started to piss off the little blond nurse from Australia to the point that she started snapping at me. It was then that I put her in her place, saying that Mom's mental condition was why we were there. With that, she finally calmed down and so did Mom.

After a long wait, we got the urine specimen to check if she had a bladder infection. That could have been the whole problem all along. Then they came out and told us they could find nothing wrong, and told me to take her to a psychiatrist. I told them we had an appointment on Thursday. I thanked them and took Mom back home to gut it out till we could see Dr. Wiley.

So there I was, sleep deprived with Mom sleeping only three to five minutes at one time. When she was awake, she'd be calling for her parents loudly, "Walter! Mom! Walter! Mom!" This would go on for hours until she would finally fall asleep by morning.

I was exhausted, but still had to work. My first customer Bob Schultz came in. Bob understood what I was going through since his mother also lived with him. I had known Bob since the early 80's and we both kind of laughed, because there we were, years later, doing the same thing.

I also had known my next client, Peter, for a long time. As I told him what I was going through, I could see the concern in his eyes. While I cut his hair, Mom started calling out for her dead parents again and I had to check on her four times. Peter rolled his eyes and said, "I hope you're doing o.k."

I told Peter, "I don't think I am."

That afternoon, Friday, a nurse from Home Healthcare, showed up. I'd forgotten I'd called her. She was paid by Medicaid and asked what I needed. I explained again the situation. As she took Mom's vitals, I told her that Mom really needed a shower and she wouldn't let me help her. Before she left, she told me to call Monday and that they'd see what they could do. Monday couldn't come soon enough; Mom smelled awful.

On Saturday, things made a turn for the worse. I didn't think they could get any worse, but, boy, was I wrong.

While I was working on clients, even during the day, I found myself having to leave them in my chair for five minutes at a time to check on Mom. It was terrible. I called my friend Donnie and had him bring his daughter Sophia over to "mommy sit." Sophia was only thirteen at the time, and was like a niece to me. Mom loved her, so she was happy to do this for Uncle John. Thank God for small miracles.

By Saturday evening, I was numb. Mom was in and out of delirium every five minutes or so. She thought I was her boyfriend as I sat on the foot of her bed. She asked if she could kiss me on the cheek. As I bent down, she grabbed the back of my head and tried to pull my face to hers and kiss me on my lips. I pulled back very quickly, and she started sobbing, saying that I didn't love her. This was just too much. I didn't understand and felt like I was feeding her pills that just weren't working.

Mom's sleep pattern continued until 1:00 a.m. Sunday morning. I was sitting at my desk, dozing off for five minutes at a time, when it grew eerily silent. After sitting there for fifteen or twenty minutes, I thought Mom may have passed out or had a stroke, so I went to check on her.

The door was open a crack, so I peered in. It was dark, but I could see a silhouette of her knees in the air with the blanket across them. She had Lil' Dog in a headlock, but he didn't seem to mind. Her left arm was moving vigorously up and down in short strokes. She was rubbing her button, masturbating. Something any son wouldn't want to see, I expect. As for Lil' Dog, it must've been like autoerotism. I then went back to my office, knowing she was ok.

When she finished, she started calling for her dead parents again. I'd check on her, and then go back to my office. Then it fell silent again and I checked on her. She was into round two, masturbating again.

This went on all night. Every hour I'd get a twenty-minute nap while she rubbed one out. By sunlight, she'd done this four times. And I thought to myself that I couldn't do that four times a night. You go, Mom. At least now I'll get some sleep.

On Sunday, she must've been exhausted. I was. She was in and out of sleep; however, I dreaded what lay ahead that evening. Even though I knew I would get some twenty-minute naps, it just wasn't right.

Before bed, Mom's sister Marilynn came over and I explained what had gone on the night before. She spent about an hour with Mom, which seemed to calm her down. When Mom finally had to go to the bathroom for a bowel movement, we helped her in and soon the house stunk to high heaven. Marilynn was gagging, and without saying a word, she left. She returned half an hour later with three cans of orange air freshener. I finally understood why Marilynn didn't step up to the plate to help with Mom like I had hoped. She couldn't stand the smell. She told me to hang in there, and then she left.

While I was at my desk on Monday, at about 1:00 a.m. the same scenario started to play out again. It looked like I'd get my twenty-minute naps once an hour like clockwork. I didn't know how Lil' Dog survived without being choked, but he did.

At five, I was suddenly awakened by Mom's crying. By the time I got to the bathroom door, she was standing there in her nightshirt, holding a newspaper between her legs and peeing everywhere. I said, "Momma, you're sick, and after a shower we're gonna get you some help."

At about eight in the morning, I called the nursing service to see what time they were coming to shower Mom. The nurse told me in a couple of days. I said I wished she would have told me that on Friday and hung up. I probably sounded rude, but I was pissed.

Mom finally agreed to a shower. So after I placed towels over the floor in the bathroom and set the water temp for her, she went into the bathroom. She didn't want me in there, so I told her to be careful.

She wasn't in the bathroom for but a minute when I heard a big thud followed by her screaming. I rushed in and she was sprawled on the floor, butt naked. I picked her up, and her skin hung on her bones like sheets on a clothesline. I helped her into the shower, turned my head away, and let her bathe. She had slipped on the floor in the only place I hadn't put a towel.

When she was finished, I was still looking away, and handed her a towel. She dried off, wrapped the towel around herself and then I helped her to her room. She got dressed on her own and then we were off to the E.R. at Valley View Hospital again.

At the ER they took us in immediately, and after they examined Mom, they told me there was nothing they could do. All I wanted was a referral to a psychiatric hospital, but they told me I'd need a psychiatric referral. I was to the point of begging; I was frustrated and exhausted.

It was then that the head nurse in records stepped in and told me to follow her to records. Down in records, the nurse retrieved Mom's file. She gave me the name of Haven Behavioral Hospital. I told her that Susan from Heritage Nursing Home had given me the name of a geriatric psychiatric hospital in Aurora, Colorado, and asked her which one she preferred. She gave me a look, like, "What are you, stupid?" I got it, and said that I guessed she preferred the one she told me about. She just looked at me and smiled; duh. I thanked her and we were on our way.

As we drove back up valley, I thought to myself how weird these procedures were. They couldn't give me a referral. It must have been to cover their butts so they wouldn't be sued if the hospital they referred me to fucked up. Lawyers again. Had this been a broken leg, it would have been easier.

I called Haven as I drove. They said they needed a referral; however they would take down all the information I could give them, and see what they could do. That gave me a little hope.

It was almost Tuesday morning, and that night was just like the previous night. Except in the morning, she was noticeably weaker. At that point, I thought that if this went on any longer, we were all gonna die, her of a stroke, me from exhaustion, and Lil' Dog of strangulation.

I called Senior Protection Services and explained my situation. They told me to take her back to the ER and just leave her if I had to. Then they'd have to do something. Scary.

So without hesitation, I loaded Mom in the car in her pajamas, and with me in mine, too, we were back down valley to the hospital.

I was ten miles from the house and by this time Mom knew how sick she was. I received a call, and it was a nurse from Haven, the psychiatric hospital in Thornton, Colorado. She said she'd look over my information and to bring Mom on in. I didn't have to think about it but for a millisecond. So we were off to Denver, pajamas and all.

CHAPTER XXII
OFF TO HEAVEN, I MEAN HAVEN!

So, there we were, Mom and I, on our way to Denver. When we left the house that morning, I thought it would be a sixty-mile drive and a couple of hour ordeal. But it was gonna turn into an eight hour drive to the Denver area and back, and we were still in our pajamas.

As I drove through Glenwood Canyon on Interstate 70, I kept reassuring Mom that everything was gonna be all right. By this point, she was so mentally delusional that it was physically taking its toll. I didn't know if she would ever recover, and as I drove, Mom would tell me she knew she was real sick and that we had to get help.

We arrived in Thornton, Colorado, a burb just north of downtown Denver. As I wheeled Mom in to check her in, I thought to myself that I might never see her again. Her current condition would probably please the people I'm fighting in court. They would be pleased that she was like this so they could claim at the next hearing that she was always this way, and that what I did during the past nine and a half months was just a big charade. In reality, it would be the self-fulfilling prophecy, the accident I talked about earlier in this book.

I rolled her up to the nurses' station, and they were expecting us since I called along the way. They took us directly to her room which had two beds, but no roommate. The nurse and I sat in chairs facing Mom, who was sitting on the bed. She got a little agitated when we removed her shoe laces, but didn't have the energy to sustain a fight.

As the nurse took all the necessary intake information, I described Mom's bizarre behavior over the last several weeks and also her masturbation episodes of the past few days. After finishing my story, I asked if this behavior was normal.

The nurse was quite frank and to the point, stating that the masturbation happened all the time, especially in women because at that age, there are more of them still living and that men that old are usually impotent. That said, I asked her what the staff did. She replied that if it happened in an inappropriate place, like the dining room, they just wheeled them back to their room and let them finish. There was no berating or telling them it was wrong or that they'd go blind. They just let them finish. I guess I did something right the last few days.

So after Mom was settled in, I realized that I was still in my pajamas and Mom didn't have any other clothes. So it was off to Wal Mart for a shopping spree.

The shopping experience was another story all together, but I figured it out and picked out summer sweat suit-like pajamas with Disney characters and some brightly colored tee-shirts for Mom. I bought a pair of jeans for myself. That would be the last thing I could afford for myself for the next year.

By the time I returned to Haven, Mom was asleep. I put the new clothes on the bed next to her and kissed her on the forehead. Then the nurse gave me a tour of the facility. Everything was painted white; it was almost sterile looking. It was very well staffed as far as I could tell, and most of the patients I saw were in different states of reality. There was even one guy dancing by himself, just like in <u>One Flew Over the Cuckoo's Nest</u>. It was a very bizarre place for me, never having been in a mental hospital. All I could hope for was that they'd take good care of Mom and make her as well as they could.

I thanked everyone and headed for the exit without Mom for the first time in ten months. I jumped into the Cougar for the four hour drive home. Soon Denver was in my rearview mirror and the mountains were in front of me and I was on I-70 headed west.

About forty-five minutes out, I was in the foothills and realized I hadn't eaten all day. So I pulled off at the Genesee exit and stumbled onto The Chart House. It was a restaurant chain a friend of mine, Herbie Balderson, had started in the 70's. There had been one in Aspen where we used to party and have dinners. They had the best prime rib I've ever had and I couldn't help but wonder if the food at this one was the same.

So I walked in and took a seat at the bar. The place smelled just like the old Chart House in Aspen that closed four or five years ago. The bartender was a young, exotic looking woman in her twenties whose name was Nicki. As I talked to her, I told her about the old days in Aspen and how the original Chart House had a brass penis for the main door handle. Most people didn't even notice it until, if it was appropriate, their server would tell them. This brought some laughs from Nicki and the people sitting near me.

After ordering my drink and prime rib, I was off to the salad bar with a crazy appetite. It was early, so the restaurant was slow, and after a few bites, I started telling Nicki about my experience, what I was going through, and that I was writing a book. I was a bit taken aback by my own behavior, spilling my guts out to a total stranger in a customer-bartender relationship. Being a hairdresser, I was usually the listener.

As I finished up my story, I'd developed a friendship with Nicki and learned she'd gone to school for communication in the broadcasting industry, but had to take a job that paid real money to support her three-year-old son. That was admirable, but Nicki was beautiful, half French and half Indian from the Dakotas, and certainly had the command of the English language to be an anchor on television.

When I was finished, I thanked her for listening to my rants and raves and told her I'd stop on my next trip through and drop off part of my book. I thanked her, and as I left, it dawned on me that I hadn't talked to anyone that normal in weeks. Oy!

I made it home by about eight o'clock that evening; it had been a very long day. As I sat in the Cougar, I looked over, and the passenger seat was empty. After all those months of taking care of Mom, watching her improve, and learning to love her, my eyes started to tear up. My little buddy, my mom, was no longer with me. I could only hope that she would survive, like the cat she is, with nine lives. I could only hope and pray that she would pull through again like she'd done before.

With Mom gone for I didn't know how long, I only had to deal with Lil' Dog, Lucky Pierre, or Devil Dog, as my brother Bill calls him. With Mom gone, he was bored; no more erotic nights, or the certainty of autoeroticism. It was time for Bill to come pick him up and take him back to his posse of Rottweilers and his Dobie girlfriend Star.

Bill decided to drive out on the July 4th weekend. I love my brother, but sometimes he's kind of a kook. That's one of the busiest driving holidays of the year, as you well know.

He made it in twenty-five hours and I met him

in Glenwood Springs in front of a music store where they were repairing my sax. I arrived first and took a seat on a street bench. Bill got there fifteen minutes later. So there I was with Lil' Dog in a strange state, and as Bill walked up the sidewalk, Lil' dog went berserk seeing his owner. How nice.

Bill took Lil' Dog in his car and followed me back to Old Snowmass. I filled him in on Mom's condition, and after one night he was ready to go home. He didn't like to be away too long.

We loaded up both cars and headed to Thornton to see Mom. It was July 4th, and not a normal visiting day. I called ahead as Mom's guardian and explained the situation, that it was the only time Bill could see his mother. They made an exception that one time, and after we arrived, they let Bill see her.

Since only one person at a time was allowed in, I waited outside, talking to a black man who had no legs and severe burns from being hit by a car in St. Louis years ago. He was being shuffled from one rehab hospital to another, and wasn't from the psych ward.

As he and I were chatting about how his life had gone, a van came to pick him up and take him downtown in his electric wheel chair. A Mercedes SUV then pulled in, and as the lady who exited the car walked up, I asked her if she worked there. She replied that she did, and in fact was the CEO of the whole hospital.

She never should have told me that because for the next ten minutes, I bent her ear and told her my story. I thanked her for taking Mom in and told her they needed to get the word out to other hospitals in Colorado what they have to offer, so someone else wouldn't have to go through what I'd gone through. I told her that if I had known about Haven earlier, I would have brought Mom there directly when she showed the first signs of medical delirium. It was nice to hear. About the time I was done thanking her, Bill appeared and informed me I could see Mom for about five minutes, so I went in.

She didn't look so hot, but a lot better than when I brought her in. After my visit, the head nurse came up to me somewhat agitated and told me they had regular visiting hours and not to expect special treatment again. With that said, I was outa there.

After my goodbyes to Bill in the parking lot, he was off with Lil' Dog back to Rockford, back to da hood, and I was off to another four hour drive back to Old Snowmass. The nice thing was, there was no dog and I'd get to stop at the Chart House and drop off the first few chapters of my book to Nicki and have another prime rib dinner. Then I was on my way home.

I kept close contact with the hospital from home. They asked me for the names of all of Mom's children and her husband for interviews. I gave them what I could and also the name of the guardian ad litem, Kim Timmerwilke, to expedite this process.

After about a week, as my life started to return to as normal as it could be, they said it was time to transfer Mom to a dementia nursing home. Finally, after arrangements were made, she was accepted to Julia Temple Nursing Home in Englewood, Colorado, a suburb on the south side of Denver.

So it was off to Denver once again to explain Mom's psychological and medical situation to the new facility. My good friend Jimmy tagged along to see how I handled this since his own mother was in a similar situation back in Boston.

I was sure Mom would be glad to see him, 'cause he's like another son to her.

We arrived at 11:30, on time for my meeting. After checking in, we were ushered into the administrator's office. As the staff came into the room, one by one, to my surprise and delight, they were all young good-looking professional women. With the exception of the all-female court back in Rockford, I almost always have had better luck communicating with the opposite sex.

The women all had different duties and would all become Mom's guardian angels on her road to recovery. Leading up the group was Jessica, a young, attractive girl in her early twenties. She had her MSW and was head of social services and would be my main contact during Mom's rehabilitation. Melissa was the head nurse in Mom's unit, which was the highest functioning unit in the facility. She has his, hers, and their children and is married to her childhood sweetheart. I wondered how she juggled her family and a job, but she was pretty amazing.

Rachel, the other head nurse in Mom's unit, was amazing as well, but I wouldn't have as much contact with her. Also in attendance was Stephanie, the dietitian who dressed like and had the looks of a model. She would help with Mom's blind loop syndrome. Beth, a very tall, lanky, blond who looked just like one of my old girlfriends, was the art, music, and activities director, which was right up Mom's alley. There was also the enforcer, Michelle, the leg-breaking money-chaser. Last, but most importantly, was Taylor, the therapy dog. Mom loved dogs and missed Lil' Dog, so Taylor, who came to work with Jessica every day, was as important as or more important than anyone in the room. And I think he knew that.

The meeting went very smoothly due to the women's

professionalism. One by one they told me their responsibilities and asked me questions as I filled them in on Mom's previous life back in Rockford. I told them about her abusive marriage, the terrible treatment she received at Alden Park Strathmoor Nursing Home, the sexual assault I read about in her diaries, and the severe beating she received at the hands of another patient which went unreported by the facility. I also explained that she received no medical or psychological care after the incident.

The women assured me that they kept a close eye on their patients, since they were well-staffed. Even though these types of situations seldom occurred, they were on top of them immediately and followed proper procedures to treat the victims.

My friend Jimmy looked on, and after the meeting told me he couldn't believe how casual and relaxed I was dealing with so many women at one time. I simply replied, "Practice."

Being satisfied Mom was in good hands, James and I headed to her unit, Sage, to see her. Jessica and Melissa walked us through all the secure doors, giving us the code and showing us how to enter and exit without letting any patients escape.

Escape; that made me think back to the institutions I've been in on this journey. With the exception of the home for the developmentally disabled, the nursing homes always had about five or six patients trying to escape. I couldn't help thinking that some of them were just like Mom, put away against their will, their rights stripped away from them, maybe because the courts or family members or both couldn't be bothered. It's a tragic situation. I can only hope that by writing this book I can create some awareness. I pray this isn't just wishful thinking on my part; maybe one man or woman, by doing what I'm doing, can cause change.

When I saw Mom for the first time after she was out of the psychiatric hospital, I was pleasantly surprised. Looking around at the other patients, I saw some catching flies, sitting on chairs with their eyes and mouths open and heads tilted back in uncomfortable positions, and others walking around aimlessly. Some came up to take my arm, probably just for some human touch. Then I saw Mom with her walker. She rolled up and gave me and then Jimmy big hugs. I'm not sure what they did at the hospital, but they brought her back.

We went into Mom's room, and she and Jimmy sat on her bed while I stood and chatted. I couldn't believe how sharp she was, considering what her condition had been three weeks before. My mind, however, was reeling from the fact that we shouldn't have had to go through this. If only the two hospital ER's in Aspen and Glenwood had policies in place to direct people to the proper facilities. But I think back now that it was probably the fear of liability of lawsuits if their referrals went awry that prevented them from making those referrals. Lawyers, again.

Even with the distrust between the health care systems and the legal systems, they are so intertwined in this quagmire, almost to the point of private industry red tape. It almost cost my mother her life.

Mom seemed happy, and even had a boyfriend named Andy. After Mom and I talked for a spell and I gave her a suitcase full of her clothes and her art supplies, her boyfriend walked in. When I first met Andy, I thought he was one of the employees. I sometimes thought that about the other patients too, and found that kinda funny. But maybe they were like Mom, a few throw-away, disposable citizens who had fallen through the cracks.

They had a beauty salon in another unit in the basement, so off we went to get Mom's hair done. I'd brought all my equipment, color and all, so I cut and colored her hair and had her looking normal again. She went back to her unit happy.

Before saying goodbye, I stopped by the nursing office and thanked Jessica, Melissa, and Rachel, and told them I couldn't believe how caring they all were, handling their patients with kid gloves. Although there were probably a lot of patients over-medicated, I told them that what they were doing was admirable, and I could tell that that it was more than a job for them; it had to be a passion.

With that done, I was ready to leave and said goodbye to Mom and her boyfriend. I turned back as I was about to go through the secured door and Mom and Andy were holding hands, smiling and waving goodbye.

So I was off to the mountains, back home. It was a four hour trip that I would make fifteen more times before November. That's a lot of driving.

On the way, Jimmy and I stopped at the Chart House for dinner and to see Nicki. I'd brought part of my book for her to read and some smoked salmon for the chef to try. Nicki was busier this time, but we still caught up on my Mom and her situation of being a single mom. After my experience with Mom, I could sympathize with her. After dinner and another three hours on the road, I was back home with no dog or Mom, just me and the solitude of my trailer. This break would give me time to write and get prepared for my next court date in Rockford on July 16th.

I couldn't be more prepared, but what happened back in Rockford would be extraordinary and a pivotal turning point in my life.

CHAPTER XXIII

JOHN MEETS JESSE

Eh, Rockford at last, I could hardly wait. It seemed crazy, but this would be my twelfth trip back and ninth time I had to go to court. I already had guardianship of person for my mother. The reason I was still in court was because of Ms Rudy and her allegations that I took my mom out of state in July of 2009. I'd answered all her accusations on her motion of "rules to show cause" and withdrew my "motion to dismiss" since both documents state basically the same argument. Up to this time, it had cost me over thirty thousand dollars in lost wages and cash money. But it was Ms Ruby, my father, and the court that had caused this case to continue, not me. All I've ever wanted was for Mom to be given her rights back and the court to order the return of her Social Security money that they'd been withholding. And all they'd wanted was to punish me financially for taking care of my mother. I just didn't get it. They know I'm doing a good job. They know; they know.

Bill picked me up from the bus, and I loaded up my luggage, and before I could get in the car, Kim Timmerwilke called me. She said, "I hope you haven't left yet; court was just cancelled again. Judge Fabiano is on vacation in Italy." I wasn't happy, to say the least. It was 4:00 p.m. on Friday, and they made the decision to tell me this late. I was pissed off. First time, shame on you; second time, shame on you. I was silent for a moment, and then asked Kim why they hadn't called me earlier. Now I travel a lot and always plan and buy my ticket ahead of time and couldn't believe the judge hadn't planned ahead. That was so wrong.

I made my displeasure known to Kim and then filled her in on Mom's current condition and said goodbye. I'm sure I was short, but thanked her anyway and told her I'd see her at the next court hearing. What a total waste of my time and money. I should have been charging them for my expenses.

Since I couldn't leave 'til Tuesday, I made the best of it. I went back to the hood house and waited for Diane to pick me up. I picked up the local paper and as I was reading it, I saw a small article about the killing of the young man named Mark Anthony Barmore in the church daycare center four blocks from the hood house. It stated that the Reverend Jesse Jackson was going to speak on Sunday at the morning service, and they'd hold a news conference in the afternoon on the grand jury's report of this incident. Now I'd been to black churches before, but not in thirty years because Aspen's fairly white, and that's an understatement. The only other time I had a chance to see Reverend Jackson was in Aspen at a fundraiser when he ran for president. However, the function was sold out, and I couldn't get a ticket.

When Di picked me up to go back to her crib where I had a bed of my own, I told her I was going to attend church to hear Jesse on Sunday and asked her if she'd like to go. She replied, "That would be interesting." So we were set to go.

There was nothing I could do till Monday about the court case, so I was on vacation for the weekend. Friday and Saturday night I spent time with the girls, Diane, Karen and Janelle, going to dinner, dancing, and letting the good times roll. We even went "chunky dunkin'," which is middle-aged chubbies hot tubbing. Sunday morning came, and Di and I got ready for church. We had breakfast—Di's a great cook—and off we went.

We arrived at Kingdom Authority Church early. I was expecting a large crowd, but when we got out of the car, there were only a few people around and a lot of press vehicles. At first I thought it might be the wrong Sunday.

As we entered the church, we were greeted by an usher who directed us to the sanctuary. We were almost the first ones there. There were a couple of young black men playing gospel music, and we took our seats in the third pew from the front. I looked to the left of the stage/pulpit and there were about nine or ten photographers and cameramen tuning their equipment for Jesse's appearance. They were mostly white.

I was expecting a large rush of people, but it didn't happen. When people finally filed in, the congregation was sparse, about forty people, mostly women and mostly black. There were only two or three other white people. It didn't make any sense.

Here we had a former American presidential candidate, like him or not, speaking at an open venue for free in a democratic city, and hardly anyone showed. Under these circumstances, with an open forum, I just didn't get it. Was the town still that racist? We're not talking about the Deep South; we're talking about the Heartland.

When the service started, it was like being at a Motown concert with a gospel soloist. It was great and extremely moving. Then the minister took the pulpit and introduced himself as Reverend Brown. During all this time, I forgot about the media being there and just took it all in as they were taking pictures and filming.

Reverend Brown apologized, saying Jesse was running late from Chicago, but would be there shortly. He then gave us the agenda for the day and went on to preach to his flock. He said from the pulpit that the number of people in his congregation had gone down fifty percent or more since the shooting at the daycare center. People just didn't feel safe; I didn't think I would either.

Reverend Brown didn't dwell on the shooting during his sermon, but preached love, acceptance, and tolerance. He supported peaceful protest, not hate, and by the time Jesse arrived, I was sincerely moved. Even though I'm not a Christian or God-fearing man, I was moved, as was Diane, who is a God-fearing woman.

Jesse finally arrived, took over the pulpit, and started to preach. I'd always had a preconceived image of the Reverend Jackson from print and too much television news. Most of the press was negative, with too many sound bytes. As he spoke, I was mesmerized. He wasn't who I thought he was; he was first and foremost a preacher, and a very good one. He wasn't doing this for the media; he was preaching to the flock. Even though there were so few of us, he was sincere when he read scripture and it was amazing. Now I'm not star-struck, as you know by now. I've spent time with heads of state, movie stars, and rock stars, but this was different. I'd like to be able to say that I was saved that day; I wasn't. But I was truly moved, which was something I'd never had happen in church before.

After his sermon and scripture reading, Jesse started talking about handguns, which surprised me. I thought he was there to talk about the Mark Anthony Barmore case. Hum.

Reverend Jackson talked about how handguns kill over 35,000 Americans a year, children and adults; bullets don't know the difference. And it's not a white or black problem;

it's an American problem. He went on to give statistics which broke it down to children shooting children, accidental shootings, and premeditated murder. We hadn't lost that many servicemen in Iraq and Afghanistan over the course of those conflicts. The statistics were staggering.

Now, I've been a gun-toting liberal most of my life and I own a handgun. It's registered, but it sits up on a closet shelf, unloaded. It's been there for years. The last time I had taken it anywhere was on a camping trip to scare off bears if I had to. Jesse was so passionate that I decided that when I returned home I'd give it to Huff, a peace officer friend of mine. I just didn't need it. I didn't live in the hood anymore. That was powerful.

When Jesse was done speaking and preaching, the flock was let go. Afterward, we went up and spoke and shook hands with Jesse, acknowledging the wonderful service. Then I took a picture of Di with Jesse with my cell phone.

Diane and I then went to Zammuto's Drive-In on the south side for lunch. Di and I split some fries and a pulled pork sandwich, topped off with our own lemon granitas. Since Zammuto's was now black–owned, I asked the girls behind the counter why they weren't at church to hear Jesse. They were surprised, saying that they didn't even know he was in town. For some reason, the media didn't publicize it much. I showed them Di's picture with Jesse on my phone and they seemed amazed and told me if we talked to him that afternoon to send him down to Zammuto's for some soul food.

We then headed back to the church for the news conference. When we got there, a line had formed to go back in, but not to the sanctuary. People were lined up on the stairs to the basement of the daycare center where Mark Anthony Barmore had lost his life in front of eleven children and the preacher's wife and daughter who were running it.

It was so hot in that room with all the cameras, lights, and people, that everyone was sweating. Jesse appeared along with a young black attorney to help with the reading of the grand jury report which had exonerated the two officers involved. I would find out later that both officer Pool and North had been involved in on-duty shootings that resulted in death before. I've known officers who, throughout their whole careers hadn't even drawn their weapons in the line of duty. I think the officers who were involved in the shooting are the exception, not the rule, but a few can make a whole department look bad.

As they stood in front of the boiler room door, Jesse spoke first, telling people that if they were to march, to be passive, no violence. He couldn't express that enough. Then he talked about the grand jury report. And the scenario of how this happened in front of children. He described how one four-year-old child was so traumatized she'd lost her hair. Psychological counseling wasn't provided for the adults and children who were present. I was in Colorado at the time of Columbine, and I remember that, for two weeks after that fatal day, the news showed the counselors working with those students and teachers. A killing's a killing; whether it's one victim or sixteen, it still had to have the same effect on people. When Jesse was finished speaking, he turned it over to the young attorney to explain what he thought was a flawed conclusion.

As he took the podium to speak, you could hear a pin drop. The report stated that Mark Anthony Barmore was wanted only for questioning in a domestic violence case for allegedly holding a knife to his girlfriend's throat, and when the officer spotted him, he ran into the church for sanctuary. I don't know why he ran, but it cost him his life and ruined many people's lives, including the officers who shot him. There were lots of victims. In that report, he went on to say that the suspect had hidden in the boiler room and was ordered to come out. A struggle for a gun occurred and it went off and grazed his face. As they held him on the floor, the next three rounds were shot almost point blank in his back. But the report contradicted itself, saying that the suspect had no gun powder residue from his hands to his shoulder; therefore there must not have been much of a struggle, if any.

It was a totally unsafe situation. The preacher's wife and daughter shielded the children the best they could with their bodies. Shooting guns in such close quarters with civilians around just seems inexcusable to me. The irony is that the way the officers shot him as he was lying on the floor, the bullets never exited his body. Due to physics, they were just three pools of lead just under the skin of his abdomen and chest. I couldn't believe what I was hearing. It was just too much.

Before he was finished, my mind wandered, as it so often does, to how unequally justice is served in our country. I was reminded of my call to jury duty in the case of Charlie Sheen in Aspen. He had been charged with holding a knife to his wife's throat and had walked out of court with the help of his sleazy attorney. We seem to have two systems: one for the haves and another for the have-nots.

We'd been down in the hot basement of the church for hours when they finally wrapped it up with a Q and A session with the press. As the group dispersed, Jesse once again called for peaceful protest and restraint.

Exhausted from the heat, we filed out. Reverend Brown was at the door when we left, and Diane and I thanked him. I told him I'd like to talk to him sometime since I was already writing a cautionary tale, and if successful, I might like to write another.

Di and I headed back to her house to cool off in her swimming pool. It was small, but it was cold and felt great. The humidity was deadly that time of year in the Midwest.

The night before, my friend Doak had called me to inform me of the passing of his mother Do Ann. I was thankful I had seen her twice that year before she died, but told Doak I probably wouldn't make it to the wake and would see him at the funeral. He went on to say that the last six weeks of Do Ann's life was hell for the family. I told him I could sympathize, and said that she had fought and battled and stayed in her own house almost to the end. I hoped my words were comforting.

I got another good night's sleep, and in the morning I had coffee as Di got ready for work. She only had to work in the morning, so we planned to go boating in the afternoon. Still upset from the cancellation of court, I decided to call the office of Illinois Attorney General, Lisa Madigan, and see if I could get through this time. I had called previously months before, only to be referred to another government agency.

This time it would be different. The attorney general had started to raid nursing homes under an operation known as Operation Guardian. They would sweep unannounced into nursing homes around the state, removing felons who were in them against Illinois rules. They targeted nursing homes where relatives had complained about the safety of their relatives who were in them. Well, my complaint must have triggered the raid at Arden Park Strathmoor.

I finally got through and was able to talk to one of the attorney general's chief investigators, Kevin O'Connell. I told Kevin my story, and he all but said that my report caused the raid. He couldn't have been any more specific as it would violate the HIPAA rule of disclosure. But I knew it was my report because my mother was the only one beaten that year at Alden Park Strathmoor. I was pleased. Before I hung up, I asked about Mom's rights and the way they violated them during her adjudication. His only advice was to contact the Colorado ombudsman since Mom now lived in Colorado. After twenty minutes or so, I thanked him for his time and said that I would probably be back in touch. I felt the conversation was productive.

Di got home around noon and we packed up for lunch on the river. It was an enjoyable cruise, and brought back memories of my water skiing days. Those were wild ones; we were young and healthy back then.

The day went fine until after we ate. Di couldn't start her boat, which was an old antique she had inherited from her boyfriend, Roger, after he passed. You still had to hand prime the motor, but the hand ball pump was cracked and we just couldn't get it to go.

It took a while, but after jerry-rigging it, we headed back down river. It would be too late for me to attend the funeral for Do Ann, but I was sure Doak and his family would be pretty overwhelmed and that I could give my condolences later. And I did.

Back at the marina, I ran into people I hadn't seen in over thirty years. When I was asked what I was doing, I filled them in on my journey so far and how I was writing a book about it. They were all very interested and voiced concern about their own relatives. I told them I'd let them know when my book came out and that maybe it would make some changes in the system and make it better.

On the way home, we stopped at Mikey's with Vito, and the four of us watched a movie Mikey had made on the river with Roger when he was alive. It was a bunch of Italian boys on the boat, Roger's posse. It was like watching the movie Good Fellas. They were busting each other's chops and giving Mikey shit for wearing a "banana hammock." And then another Mike, a schoolteacher at my old high school, gave a monologue about an incident as a hallway monitor during lunch. As he spoke, Roger would turn up the radio louder, just to irritate him. I almost fell on the floor from laughter. I hadn't laughed that hard in years.

Soon after, we left and headed back to Diane's. She hadn't been able to watch those videos since Roger had taken his own life. She told me how Roger had gotten to that point and what she'd done to try to save him. The story was so sad and unbelievable. It took place at the same hospital my Mom was taken to when she called 911 on my father in April of 2009. Roger had become depressed and was on medication that would take thirty days to kick in. He knew he wasn't getting better and sought help at the psychiatric ward, only to be turned away and told to give the medicine a few more days. Roger didn't make it. It was tragic. I thought how inept those people who work there must be; he didn't have to die.

When Di was finished telling me the story, we both had tears rolling down our cheeks. We were both tired, so it was off to bed, since I was leaving the next day.

The morning came too quickly. After coffee and breakfast, I hustled to Bill's barber shop to grab his car. I had one more errand to run. I couldn't thank Diane enough, and after hugs and kisses, I was off to the Visiting Nurse Association.

This was my second visit to this agency. The previous visit was to fill them in on my father and mother's relationship. They seemed concerned, but I only got vague answers.

This time would be different; since I was Mom's guardian, they would have to comply and give me the records upon request. As far as I could tell, it was the only good thing about being a guardian.

The same woman with whom I talked on my first visit came out. When I asked her for Mom's records, she said I'd have to email my request. I thought that was odd, but asked for her business card. She said she didn't have one, but would jot down her information for me. She tore off a corner of a piece of stationery and wrote her name and email down. When she handed me the piece of paper, the letterhead read Alden Healthcare. My jaw nearly hit the floor. The stationery was from the parent company that owned Alden Park Strathmoor.

I quickly thanked them and made a hasty retreat. As I drove away, my mind was swirling again. Could this be another link? The Visiting Nurse Association is supposed to be unbiased and independent. Were they connected too? I couldn't figure out why, if they found Mom's home unsafe and unclean for her, it was ok for my elderly father to stay in it; he was the hoarder. Scary, huh? I didn't know who to trust.

I went back to Di's, loaded my luggage in the car, and drove off to get Bill to drop me at the bus. I showed him the stationery with Alden Healthcare Systems on it. He just looked at it and shook his head. So it was back to Aspen.

It would be two months before I had to return to Rockford for court; however, I was only back in Aspen for a few days when Kim Timmerwilke, the guardian ad litem, called and told me there would be a hearing on July 26, 2010. But since I was just there for the hearing that wasn't, they'd waive the policy that would have had me return and let me appear by phone. The way the courts had handled the case so far, I should have been able to do this all along. It would have saved me a lot of wasted time and money. Deep down, I think they thought I'd lose this war of attrition and not be able to outlast them and just go away. That ain't happening.

The only thing that came out of the hearing by phone was an apology from the judge for not giving me ample notice. And the lawyers got to rack up their bills. This was out of control.

So for the next twelve weeks, I made my 400 mile round trip to Denver to see Mom. Jessica would give me progress reports on her mental health and Melissa, her nurse, would update me on her physical health. These young women knew their stuff and truly cared. Jessica informed me that Mom was functioning at the highest level in the facility and said that we could start looking at alternatives, such as assisted living.

We did have incidents, however. During the Jazz Fest in Aspen, a friend of mine, Margeaux, came to town to see her good friend Carol Chase, a singer with The Lynyrd Skynyrd Band, perform, and asked if I could do both their hair before the concert. I obliged and they paid me handsomely. Carol loved her hair, saying it was the haircut she'd always wanted and that I made her look like the rock star she is. Margeax loved hers, too. They also read chapters in my unfinished book.

When I was almost finished and was packing up my equipment, I received a call from Julia Temple Nursing Home. Apparently, Mom had been assaulted again. She must have a sharp tongue. It was nothing more than a hard slap on her back, but they immediately brought in a psychologist to make sure she was ok I thought this was the way it should be done. I thanked them for their concern; however I did miss the concert waiting for the psychologist to call after his evaluation.

Also on those trips to Denver, when I could afford it, I'd stop at the Chart House and see Nicki. It became a routine.

There were only a few days left before my return to Rockford for what would turn out to be my last court appearance, and I was ready. I'm going back to Rockford; I hope they're ready for me.

CHAPTER XXIV
SHAME ON YOU, MS RUDY

At last my day had arrived, my court day. I had a fresh haircut, a clean suit, and was ready to go. By then I was carrying an attaché case and one complete cardboard file box. I had every report possible with me, from the initial report from Swedish American Hospital to the last report from Haven Behavioral Unit. The latter had intake interviews from my brother David and my sister.

Those interviews were haunting. When asked about our home life as youngsters, David admitted our father had physically abused us as we were growing up. The interviewer stated that my sister was agitated, uncooperative, and somewhat paranoid, and my father declined to participate. This should have shown the court that something was very wrong. I believed that Kim Timmerwilke, the guardian ad litem, also obtained those records, since I'd given her Haven's number so she could get them. I didn't know if she'd read them, though. If she had, I hoped she'd passed it on to Judge Fabiano. That's her job, to seek out and obtain information in a non-biased way. I only hope she had.

Knowing this court date would be the finale, Bill also attended. He helped carry my files and was there for support. We made our way into the courtroom early, and I wondered if my father would show up. He hadn't ever before, I think mostly because he knew I was right, and he wouldn't want to answer questions about his abusive behavior throughout our lives.

Bill and I sat and talked for about ten minutes when Ms Rudy arrived. As she walked in, to my surprise, my father followed, then my brother David with two of his children. I thought to myself, what could he testify to? He had two orders of protection filed against him by his soon to be ex-wife. I could only hope he hadn't passed his behavior on to his boys. Then my sister and my father's half-sister Pam arrived. He had his posse; how nice.

Since Bill and I were sitting on the other side of the aisle, we were separated from them. As we looked back at our other family members, they wouldn't even look at us or acknowledge us. They just talked and laughed with each other as if we weren't there.

Ms Rudy, Ms Timmerwilke, and I were called to approach the bench. As I walked up with my files, Ms Rudy looked at what I had in my hands and said something to the judge. It was then that she asked if I was willing to go into Judge's chambers and talk. I thought quickly and I agreed. You're allowed to express yourself freely in Judge's chambers; maybe I could save this family, or whatever you wanna call it, the embarrassment of the evidence I'd acquired.

We all took seats in comfortable chairs with the judge at her desk. This was supposed to be more like arbitration than a court hearing.

I spoke first and described briefly what had happened to Mom after she had broken her hip and how she finally was improving. I continued by telling the women that I thought Mom could go to assisted living, but it would have to be a secured facility for her safely. Kim Timmerwilke interjected by asking if I had any problem with placing her in Rockford. I hesitated, then told her no, as long as I got to approve the facilities. But if I didn't like them, Mom wouldn't be coming back.

It was then that I brought up my father's irresponsible behavior with Mom's health insurance while he was guardian. Before I could finish, Ms Rudy objected. I truly believed at that point that she objected to my mere existence. I was frustrated; even in judge's chamber I wasn't able to present one fact at all. All my work for naught.

I then mentioned that my father had never attempted to contact his wife. To which Kim Timmerwilked replied that the last time she talked to Mom, she said she didn't care to talk to him. Kim didn't know, but Mom hadn't said "never," just not at that time. I felt like I was being stuffed, shut down. And I was.

The conversation quickly turned. Ms. Rudy wanted to know how she was gonna get paid and also spoke for Kim. I couldn't believe this. We hadn't even addressed my answers in the "rule to show cause" motion, and to this day I don't believe the judge ever read them. If she had, she would've had questions for me. I didn't think she could really be that obtuse.

By this time, every time I spoke, I felt like I was juggling dynamite and giving off sparks. I mentioned something about my former house on Belmont Blvd., how I was about to file a lis pendens since my parents had forged my signature so I could put Mom back in it. Ms Rudy looked up and rolled her eyes. Then it looked like a light went on in her head and she said she'd just attached a lien against the house for the amount she said my mother would owe. I didn't show it, but I was getting upset.

Ms Rudy had entered this case on behalf of Mother to sue as a poor person, and now, after this case is over, she is going after what little Mom has left to live out her life. How sick is that? A poor person means without funds. I guess that doesn't include property.

I felt like I was in a kangaroo court. The next thing I brought up was her back Social Security checks that Ms Rudy was supposed to obtain from my father. Again her eyes lit up as she spoke to the judge and Ms Timmerwilke, saying that they could use them to help pay Mom's part. This was an abomination. It would mean Mom would have to go without teeth. This made her look like a Jack o'lantern, and impaired her digestive system and health. My stomach did flip flops. And as I sat there steaming, my eyes darting from one woman to the other, I thought, how could they do this, withhold her Social Security for a year and then make it appear for their own purposes? It also violated federal law and the state laws don't supersede them.

It got to where I was getting reluctant to speak, 'cause every time I did, it gave Ms Rudy another idea of a way to obtain her fees. Then it came to how much I should pay. They came up with a figure of about $5000. I told the judge I didn't agree with her decision. I was basically being fined for kidnapping my mother when all I really did was save a woman's life. They might as well have been deaf.

Since I had limited funds, they decided that I'd pay Kim Timmerwilke first, at a rate of $50 a month, until her $1,600 fees were paid. I'd then pay $3,600 to Ms. Rudy, I guess for any inconvenience I might have caused her, again at $50 a month until they were paid. It was a court order, not something I would do voluntarily. Again I found myself wondering how Ms Rudy could sleep at night, knowing that what she did would directly impact my mother's health, with her walking around with no teeth. This was a woman who is a self-proclaimed advocate of elder rights. I've read her bio; I've studied everything I could find on the internet about her. Her speaking engagements, her positions on advisory committees, hell, it's all on elder rights. She doesn't practice what she preaches, au contraire, quite the opposite, because she's trampled on Mom's rights from the beginning. With the evidence, both verbal and in reports that I'd given to Ms Timmerwilke, I possible could've proven complicity between my father and Ms Rudy, had I been able to present it in court.

I let the ladies of the court know I'd spoken to the attorney general's office about Mom's case and that they all but told me, due to the HIPAA Act, that the raid on Alden Park Strathmoor was a direct result of my mother's brutal beating. They further stated that it was reports from people like me that caused this investigation. Ms Rudy again rolled her eyes back like she'd done before and muttered rather sarcastically, "Yeah, sure," as if she didn't believe me.

After thanking the judge for her time, I said that when I was growing up, I had lived across the street from some Fabianos. She stated she was already aware of that. That was funny; I hadn't mentioned it before. Maybe someone else had already played that card. I didn't know.

I walked back out of Judge Fabiano's chambers, past my father and his posse of family members. None of them would make eye contact with me, and I thought that all this court did today was weaken a family and leave it shattered. What they do is fucked. I'm not so much angry as I am totally disgusted.

This whole process had taken forty-five minutes. It was over. I wouldn't appeal; there was no reason to, not in this district, not in this court.

I met Kim outside the courtroom and asked her for her address and how to make out her check. She said, "You look angry." I replied, "No, just extremely disgusted." But I told her I was glad the case was finally over. I could grow my hair back, no more suit, no more charade as a faux lawyer. What a relief. Kim did respond by saying that I didn't have to cut my hair or wear a suit, to which I responded that I did it out of respect for the court. Oh well.

I thanked Kim this time for the 60% of what she had done, not the 40% she didn't, said goodbye, and then I was off for a drink with the girls.

Bill had gone ahead of me so I met him at his shop and told him in a nutshell what had happened in the Judge's chamber. He was pretty upset and disgusted also. Then he went on to tell me how agonizing it was to sit fifteen feet away from his own flesh and blood and be completely ignored. I think he had it tougher than I did. I said goodbye, hopped in the Cougar, and drove to the restaurant. I just wanted to drown my pain in a martini glass.

I'm sure I wasn't very good company for the girls at lunch; I was numb. But what they did to me in court only lit the fires of passion to continue to write my book and get the truth out as to what goes down in our legal and healthcare systems every day. My mother's case isn't unique. It may not have played out well, the way I did it, but our system allows this to continue every day. For every Winifred Carol Wyman that this happens to, there are ten elders out there who fall between the cracks. Without an advocate, like I've been, the abuse goes unreported. As baby boomers move into this phase in their lives, I'm afraid it will only get worse if we don't stop it now. We have the power, people.

After lunch, I went back to Bill's after I had changed back to jeans, a tee-shirt, and hat. At his shop earlier that morning, I'd run into Bob Aten, a friend of my parents. By now, Bob knew a little bit about Mom's situation, but didn't say anything. However, he told me his daughter Deborah had asked about me, so I gave him my phone number. She called, and I told her I'd meet her after lunch. So there I was. Her mother Dot had been one of Mom's best friends, and I had done Dot and Deborah's hair when I had a salon in Rockford. We had also gone to the same church in our youth, so I thought it would be fun to catch up with her after forty years.

I met her out in back of Bill's shop and as we sat on a picnic table, we quickly caught up to speed. She told me how her life had gone, how her mother had passed on, and how her dad was doing, since Bob was a man of few words. I told her about Mom's whole ordeal and that I didn't think that I could take that good of care of her again, and that she might be bound for assisted living. Deb, being a Christian girl, said she' put it into prayer. That was good, since I seemed to need some sort of higher power. At about the time I was thanking her for her prayers, Bill appeared and asked if I was ready to go to my nephew Matt's football game and invited Deb to go along.

We went to the game. I hadn't been to one in years, and it was a great time, even though Matt's team lost. On the ride back home to drop Deb off, she talked more about Mom's situation and asked me if she came out to take care of Mom, I'd bring her home. I said I would but couldn't understand how we could make it work. I wasn't sure of how much care Mom would need. Again, as we dropped her off, Deb said she'd put it into prayer.

After dropping her off, Bill took me to Di's house and left me. It would be my last night in town and the last time I'd stay at Di's on this journey of mine. She'd been such an angel, but this was the end of my frequent trips back to Rockford.

After breakfast, I loaded up the Cougar, said my good-byes to Di, and then drove down to Bill's shop.

As I bid the north end farewell, I turned to Bill and

said, "It's over. You won't see me as often anymore." We gave each other a hug and I was outta there. I lit a joint, settled in the Cougar, and was off for a twenty-four hour cruise back to Aspen. This trip would turn out to be difficult and funny, to say the least. I would need divine intervention.

That's the end of the court case, but not the end of the story.

PART III

CHAPTER XXV
DIVINE INTERVENTION

I took the long way home, diverting to the south side of Chicago for dinner with Robin's family. Gotta get my pizza fix. They're all there, her father, her brother, her sister-in-law, and my boys. After dinner, they asked how my court case went and what I was going to do with Mom. I told them that after checking out assisted living facilities in Rockford, I was pretty sure I'd be taking Mom back to Aspen for round two, yes, living with me again. I didn't know when she'd see her family again.

This side trip added about three hours onto my trip. David, Robin's brother, asked me if I'd like to get some sleep before I embarked on my journey. I thanked him for the offer and assured him I was wide awake. I thanked them for a lovely time and was off. It was 9:00 p.m.

The first nine hours of my drive were uneventful. The drive gave me time to reflect on all I had done for the last year and a half. I took a toke off a spliff, set the cruise, and drove into a fog.

I was in western Iowa. It was 4:00 a.m., and I'd just made a gas stop thirty miles from the Nebraska border. As I drove, someone pulled the shade down on the full moon and I was in thick fog. It was a good thing I was the only one on the road. I was driving through a stretch of I-80 that had wind farms on both sides of the interstate. As I looked around, it was surreal, and I felt like I was on another planet. And it wasn't the pot. Those tall towers painted white had red lights blinking for aircraft to see. But in the fog, they looked like strobe lights that left those huge blades standing still in all sorts of varying positions. This went on for as far as the eye could see. Too cool.

As I took all of this in at seventy miles an hour, it happened. I had a catastrophic blow-out on my left rear tire. Sparks were flying as I slowed down and pulled off the road to the shoulder. I got out of the car, checked the tire, and saw that it was shredded. There I was, on the side of the interstate in a thick fog, not a safe place. So I got back in the Cougar and drove real slowly for about a mile and a half on the shoulder to the next exit.

I got off at Beebeetown, Iowa, and went down the ramp. There was nothing there except a well-drilling company about a quarter mile away. The buildings were dark and no one was there. So I parked the car on the side of the entrance ramp headed west. The fog was so thick that I decided to take a nap. I slept in the car for about an hour, and as the fog started to lift at about 5:00 a.m., I decided to try to change the tire. But before I could do this, nature called, I mean nature. I had to poo, and there was nowhere to go, no trees, bushes, or buildings; no place to hide. So I decided to wing it. Since I'd done a lot of camping in Colorado, you'd think I'd have this down. Not. The few times this had happened in my life, it didn't turn out so well. But this time I had an idea. I leaned against the car on the right rear quarter panel in a sitting position, with TP in hand and voila, it worked. No mess. That done, I decided to change the tire.

I took the donut tire out and it was almost flat, but I had to use it anyway. So on it went. The only problem was I was downwind from my poo, and I was hoping that no one would stop to help. It was now 6:00 a.m. and a few cars stopped by and offered. Then a truck stopped and a young guy got out. I put my hands up and told him that I was ok. He must've thought I was crazy. I was just trying to save his olfactory nerves and my embarrassment of my poo. And I didn't think mine stunk. With that done, I was off to find a gas station for some air, driving very slowly with the four-way flashers on.

After filling the tire, it was six-thirty in the morning and nothing was open, so I decided to try to make it to a Big O Tires in Grand Island, Nebraska, by nine. The boys at the Big O were funny, trying to sell me a set of tires. I finally asked if I could buy one, and they said of course, so I bought a used one for $35. I said that sure beat $400.

Then I was on the final leg home. Since I left some of my equipment at Brandi's when I did her hair on the trip out, I stopped and got it. About a block away from her house, the Cougar died. It wasn't getting enough gas. So I got it to start every five minutes, would drive it three blocks, and it'd die again. After doing this four or five times, I was able to nurse it to a service station, where I'd be able to pick it up in a day. It was a fuel sensor gauge. I called Brandi's house, where I just was, and she gave me a ride to Julia Temple Nursing Home to see Mom.

At Julia Temple, I spent the day with Mom, and she was doing great. The girls Jessica and Melissa told me she'd be better off in assisted living or back home. At this point, I didn't know if I was up to the task of taking care of her, but I knew I couldn't leave her there much longer. It would stifle her recovery.

Mom and I walked a block to a pizza parlor for lunch and talked about what she wanted. The girls at Julia Temple had taken Mom to The Chateau, the assisted living attached to the nursing home. It was pleasant enough, small like a boutique hotel. Also, it was secured assisted living, something I'd looked for but hadn't come across in my research. Mom, however, didn't seem to fit. It wasn't that she was an elopement risk as much as she didn't want to be separated from her boyfriend, Andy. Summer love, I guessed. How nice it was for her to have a man around who wasn't abusive. How different would she have been if she'd married a man that didn't beat her. We'll never know.

Returning to the nursing home, I was told that Michelle in finance wanted to see me. I went to the basement office which was close to the main kitchen where they were working away. I was surprised at how sanitary it was, as it should be.

In Michelle's office, she told me for the first time that they needed Mom's Social Security checks from July through November. I told her I didn't have them, that they had gone directly into my account to take care of mother's expenses. She then went on to explain how the money follows the person by federal law and that I'd have to write a check to Julia Temple for $1800. I didn't have it. I asked what would happen if I didn't relinquish it. She said she'd have to turn it over to the Social Security Administration for investigation. I decided to pay it and this institution would work with me on payments. I had no problem with this but I couldn't understand how the judge and Ms Rudy back in Rockford could think they could violate federal law in district court by keeping her Social Security checks for payment of Ms Rudy's fees in 2009. But they had.

About that time I received a call that my car was ready, so I thanked all the girls and said goodbye to Mom and her boyfriend. I picked up the Cougar and headed back to the mountains.

It was sunset, a beautiful time to be driving, and about an hour into my trip my phone rang. It was Deb Aten from

Rockford. She said she'd put my request to help take care of Mom in prayer and that she would help if it were in Rockford. I said that I didn't think that would work unless I could get Mom back in her own home. But my father had moved back there, so that wasn't happening. I further stated that if I brought Mom back to Aspen, I'd have to have a commitment from Deb 'cause I couldn't do it alone. With that said, Deb told me she'd put that into prayer; she sure does pray a lot. I'm glad someone does.

Also, I wanted to keep Mom in Denver at Julia Temple for a few more weeks so she could get her new teeth. That's another problem with Medicaid; they'll only pick up the dental tab while a person is in a facility, but not when they're out. I didn't understand this either. The needs are still the same. This is also something that needs to be changed.

A week after I was home, I received mail from Ms Rudy. It was a breakdown of her bill. There were charges for talking to my sister, my father, my brother David, and the district attorney trying to have kidnapping charges filed against me. She even charged me for the motion she filed initially to start this case in May of 2009 in which she had accused me in the courtroom of copying verbatim which actually was a copy of a draft that my attorney J.F. Heckinger had sent me, but I refused to use. I copied it so I could speak in court months later. This same document, I don't know which lawyer produced it, but both had charged me for it. I call that collusion.

There weren't any phone calls from me, only from my family or ex-attorney. Ms Rudy basically had carte blanche to bill however she wanted. Not one of her charges had to do with the well-being of my mother.

To add insult to injury, she also enclosed her bill stamped in red ink "Past Due." Again Ms. Rudy must not have been in the same judge's chambers because it was agreed upon that I was to pay Kim off first, then Ms Rudy. This was pretty frustrating, to say the least.

Well, while I was waiting for the outcome of Mom's getting her teeth, a call came in from Jessica at Julia Temple. They'd found Mom on the floor in her room. She told me Mom had either been beaten again by another man in a wheelchair, or she had fallen. She was ok, but they were checking her out and would get back to me on what had happened.

It turned out that Mom had been run over by a man in the wheelchair on purpose and that they'd taken the appropriate actions. I told Jessica that I thought I'd better bring her home, and she agreed. This had to work, although they still hadn't finished her dental work.

Soon after I got off the phone with Jessica, Deb called from Rockford. God had answered her prayers, and I guess mine too. She said she'd come out to help with Mom so I could take her home and finish my book, but it'd be about two weeks before she could leave. It looked like I was getting another guardian angel.

Deb arrived. I've known her since childhood, but I really didn't know her that well. So after picking her up at the Aspen Airport, we headed down valley to the trailer. It always amazes me when friends come to visit and see how spectacular the mountain scenery is. I think it's the Rocky Mountain High.

At the trailer for the next five days I continued to write as Deb set up the bedroom for her and Mom and told me she'd even share the bed. How nice that Mom gets a roommate.

Once everything was in place, Deb and I made the trek to Denver to fetch Mom. Mom and Deb hadn't seen each other in years, but they hit it off great. Mom would now have a fulltime female friend to confide in. In fact, every morning I could hear the girls having pillow talks. It didn't get any better than that.

And in the ensuing weeks, they'd go to mommy daycare, the senior lunch program, and church every Sunday. We had Thanksgiving with Mom's sister, Marilyn, and her family, and attended the X-Games. It was a relief to see that we were all having a super time.

One night we went to see the fireworks on Aspen Mountain. I've seen this display myself fifty or sixty times, but it's always spectacular with the mountains as a backdrop, as you can imagine. Both Mom and Deb took it all in with amazed looks on their faces, like little children.

A week before Christmas, Mom got a new internist, Dr. Mizner. We couldn't have done better if we had tried. She was about as thorough a doctor as you could find. She spent an hour and fifteen minutes with Mom, Deb, and me taking her own input information. She was top shelf. She also gave me another referral to Dr. Wiley, the psychiatrist, and that was truly what we were there for, since Mom was on a low dose of Seroquel and still had that empty gaze in her eyes occasionally. But we couldn't see Dr. Wiley for another ten days. Those ten days would go by quickly. With Christmas and all, a lot would happen.

On the Friday before Christmas Sunday, I received a frantic call from brother Bill back in Rockford. Apparently, my father had had some sort of seizure and the ambulance was at his house. One of the neighbors had called Bill asking what to do and where to send him. But due to the orders of protection that they had filed against Bill and the rest of his family, Bill felt helpless. There was nothing he could do. It was ironic that my father ended up like that, shunning the very people who could help him in Rockford. I know that will sound cold, but he had made his bed with the advice of Ms Rudy and the direction of the court. Now he found himself sleeping in it.

So he was off to the hospital and then, I suppose, off to a nursing home. He hadn't, and probably never will, return to his home, and it will sit vacant just like the last house on Winnebago Street until it falls into disrepair. The lawyers continue to rack up more fees and add to the liens on that house until there will be no equity left. That's why they call them probate sharks.

On the Sunday before Christmas I dropped off Mom and Deb at church while I went out to chase the dollar and do hair. Upon my return to church, the girls were waiting by the door. I usually had to go inside and get them. When I helped them into the truck and asked why they were waiting, Mom replied that the art exhibit in the church contained more nude photos and if I'd gone in, they were afraid I wouldn't leave. She still possesses a sense of humor.

I wasn't going to be busy with clients over Christmas, so we decided to drive the Toyota truck my friend Peter sold/ gave me for fifty dollars a month so we wouldn't have to drive that Cougar through another winter. It ended up being one of the snowiest on record.

It would be a quick trip, so we'd be back by New Year's. We took off late on the twenty-first of December, 2010, on a road trip I won't soon forget. All was well except for the high mountain passes on I-70. It cleared up in Denver and was o.k. until I hit fog in Nebraska. We'd made our usual pee stops, which were much easier with Deb along for the ride. For the life of me, I couldn't figure out how she stuffed herself behind my seat. Even though it was a crew cab, it was still a small truck.

The fog would last until midway through Iowa; then it turned into the worst blizzard they'd seen in that area since the blizzard of '79. It was a harrowing drive; I'd never seen so many accidents and cars in the ditch, but we trudged on slowly with our studded snow tires and our four wheel drive. Peter was right about having the proper vehicle.

We finally arrived in Rockford, and I dropped Mom and Deb off at Deb's father's house and went to the hood house for some sleep. The next day I'd head to the Southside of Chicago for the holidays with my girlfriend and her family.

Heading in on I-90, I stopped again at Rolling Meadows to see Joey at the home for the developmentally disabled. Roxy had sent five presents and some more clothes. Joey was so happy to see me that she immediately said, "McDonald. We go McDonald." She'd remembered; how sweet. And I'd made the proper arrangements beforehand, so off we went to "McDonald."

Joey had a hearty appetite, and I told her that she could have two of everything, and she did. She was a lovely lunch date and kept me laughing with her as I taped the whole lunch on video for "Fobbi" and Mary Ann.

After lunch, it was back to the facility for Joey's Christmas. She got plenty, some new, some used, and all along I kept the video rollin'. Just being there with her and all her love made this the best Christmas I'd had in all my memories. I was flying higher with emotions than she was, I think.

When it was time for me to go, Joey wanted to come with me. I told her next time. She gave me a huge hug and I was on my way to Robin's.

It was nice to spend time with my girl and her family.

David's mother-in-law Liz was out of the rehab facility. I'd seen her in June of that summer, and she was doing well, considering she was recovering from a benign tumor. And the rest of the clan was happy to see me.

Jennifer, Robin's sister-in-law, and her nephew Ben both took interest in and read the transcript of what I had finished of my book so far. They looked captivated as they read, finding out things about their Uncle John that they didn't know, because I bared a good part of myself in that first part. After they finished, Jennifer and Ben, with wide eyes, said that they looked forward to reading the rest.

Christmas with Robin's family would be too short. I got a call Christmas afternoon from Deb telling me that Mom had to go to the hospital by ambulance at 11:00 p.m. on Christmas Eve. But she was ok. Apparently Mom and Deb had come down with a terrible flu within an hour of each other, and both of them were going at both ends in one bathroom, not a pretty sight. But Deb kept it together enough to get Mom and herself cleaned up.

Mom was weak and had no strength, and neither did Deb. They were both on the floor, trying to make it to the bed, when Deb called out to Mom to "crawl, crawl like a dog," and Mom did. About an hour after getting Mom in bed and lying next to her, she could tell that Mom wasn't doing so well. So she called an ambulance to take her to Swedish American Hospital, the same place she'd been in the psyche ward in April, 2009.

I asked Deb if I should come to Rockford right away, but she said no, to stay overnight. I then called the hospital for an update. They assured me that Mom was doing better. Merry Christmas.

The next morning, I headed back up to Rockford. It

was Mom's birthday and she was coming out of the hospital. Her doctor had called to give me the update and out of curiosity I asked him how she'd been as a patient. What he said floored me. He said Mom was cooperative and involved in her medical decisions. I asked the doctor if he would put that in writing, and he did. So here, a year and a half after being put away against her will, she was making her own medical decisions. How wrong could those courts have been?

Mom was a little slowed when I picked her up. After a short birthday party for her, I dropped her off at Deb's house for some rest. We were heading back to Colorado the next day, so I wanted her stronger for the drive home.

On December 27th, I was up early and loaded up the Beast. That's what we called the truck since it plowed on through the blizzard on the way to Rockford. I hoped it would take us home safely.

There was nothing to do but pick up some spliffs for the road and fetch Mom and Deb for the long ride home. With Deb stuffed in the back and Mom nestled in blankets next to me for the duration, we were on our way.

I swung by Bill's shop to say goodbye to the boys, and then, at Mom's request, we were off to drive by her house. It sat there empty, with Dad in a nursing home. Maybe they were just going to let it fall into disrepair. So I decided to call Kim Timmerwilke one last time to ask if it was possible to place Mom back in her own house.

Kim reiterated that the house was unfit for Mom to live in. I still didn't understand that, since they allowed my father to stay there. It was empty now; it just wasn't right. Maybe it's their liens for their fees. Maybe they plannned to force a sale. I didn't know. I could only speculate at that point. I told Kim I'd see her in April, to which she replied that I didn't have to appear; I just had to file an annual report. I was already paying her and taking care of Mom. What a fucking hassle. But that's the way it goes.

With the roads now clear, the trip back to Aspen was uneventful. We stopped a few times here and there for life's necessities, and I played my toke a joint game. We made it home safely for New Year's, fireworks and all. Happy New Year!

CHAPTER XXVI
THANK YOU JANET BEDIN AND DR. WILEY

The day finally arrived; Mom got to see her shrink, Dr. Wiley. What happened next blew me away. She was supposed to have seen him seven months before, but that was June, 2010, and we never made it, as you know. But I think it was worth the wait.

Dr. Gail Mizner, who had given Mom her second referral to Dr. Wiley, didn't like the medication she was on. Mom was too lethargic and kind of empty. But that was all to change, and change suddenly!

Dr. Wiley was a man about my age, and Deb and I sat in on Mom's session to support her. He was soft spoken and kind to Mom during the oral exam, the mini-dementia test. She didn't get frustrated or agitated, but she didn't do too well, either. She only got ten out of thirty exercises. Not good.

So after the exam, Dr. Wiley figured out a plan of attack. He totally changed all her medications. He took her off Seroquel, and put her on Aricept and a combination mood elevator and sleep aid. Bingo! After only a couple of days, it was like someone turned the lights back on as Deb and I watched her progress back at home in total amazement.

But the Aricept came with an odiferous side effect, and that was bowel incontinence that could last up to three weeks.

Mom had so little time from when her brain told her she had to go to the bathroom to when she actually got there, that she had a fifty-fifty chance of making it. But we managed to gut it out.

I called Dr. Wiley during this time to thank him profusely and to ask about the bowel movement issue. He told me we could try something else, but with Mom doing so well, I told the doc we'd stay the course. However, I had one more question for Dr. Wiley, and that was if her improvement was due to being off Seroquel or being on Aricept. He didn't know for sure, but suspected that since the turnaround was so quick, it was probably due to being off the Seroquel. I thanked him and told him he'd saved Mom again and that we'd see him in a couple of weeks.

Seroquel, the drug Dr. Wiley just took Mom off, is similar to the Risperdal Mom had been on as a chemical restraint. I was talking to a female doctor at church, and she said she was pretty sure that Risperdal had accelerated her mother's death and also caused her sister to commit suicide. Another friend of mine said that when her husband had suffered a breakdown, he kept telling her that the pills were killing him. She immediately removed him from the facility and at the time I was talking to her, he had fully recovered. These are just bad drugs, specifically prescribed off label to elders, not for what they were approved for, but where big pharma makes the biggest profits.

For the next ten days, with Mom's rapid improvement, her life would become more enjoyable. The senior center Tuesday and Thursday for greet and eat, church on Sundays, and going shopping with Deb in Aspen were pleasant activities for her. She was normal, engaging, and had her sense of humor back. It was great, and the poo's subsided. I couldn't ask for a better ending. She was back. But on January 15th, the only fear I had left happened.

All court orders of protection were still in place, and as we drove up to a parking spot at City Market, I saw my nephew, Josh, and so did Mom. Before I could stop her, she was out of the truck and making a beeline to her grandson. Unbeknownst to me, my sister was sitting in her car talking to her son. Deb squeezed out of the back of the truck and followed Mom. Because of those court orders, I couldn't join them for fear the situation would be misconstrued and I would be charged with attempting to make contact through a third party, which is a felony.

So I sat back in my seat and watched the scene unfold through my rearview mirror. My nephew was kind enough to talk to his grandma; however, he was reluctant to hug her since my sister was there and would certainly get upset.

As Mom talked to Josh, Deb was talking to my sister. My sister had known Deb through church all her life and had also sold Deb Amway products in the day. As Deb talked to her, she sat in her car, stoic, looking straight forward as if Deb weren't there. To make matters worse, when Mom tried to communicate with her only daughter, my sister just looked straight ahead, never acknowledging her own mother, the very woman who had given her life. It was sick.

After this chance meeting in the parking lot that day, Mom cried. She just couldn't understand how her only daughter could do that to her. She was upset for a month. My only thoughts were that I hoped my nephew, Josh, would have the courage to break this cycle of insanity, if not for his grandma, then at least for his children.

You would think that, regardless of how my sister felt about me, she'd have had enough decency to communicate and to get out of her car to hug our own mother. It would have meant so much to Mom.

Later that night, after the girls had settled in bed for the night, I went back to my office and turned on my computer for a little more research. I hadn't turned it on since Christmas, but now I typed in Sharon Rudy's name to retrieve some more information. Bingo, I hit the jack-pot, something that would validate what I suspected was going on in the 17th Judicial District of Illinois, with judges, lawyers, public guardians, and guardians ad litem.

Enter Janet Bedin, all over the internet: WGN News, Chicago Tribune, and WIFR Television Station in Rockford. Apparently, in conjunction with Northwestern Hospital in Chicago, the 17th Judicial District in Rockford with Ms Rudy leading the charge, were trying to take Ms Bedin's power of attorney rights for her mother, Delores, away from her. They charged that she was unfit, and they wanted to appoint a public guardian, Ms Rudy. However, they chose to mess with the wrong woman, Janet Bedin.

This woman had a lot of fight and the good fortune of hiring the right attorney, 'cause I can tell you it's hit or miss from my own experience with J.F.

The story unfolded as my eyes scanned the computer, and I was flabbergasted, but not surprised. Even though Janet's story was very different from mine, the end results for the people trying to do this to her and her mother would be the same, to profit at the expense of another family.

Janet's mom had been hospitalized for some time. Test results from x-rays taken in April, 2010, had revealed a large mass in Delores' abdomen. However, Janet wasn't informed of this until September 2010. Her mother had pancreatic cancer, and now they were trying to take her power of attorney away from her. The hospital apparently had run into money problems with Delores, and her Medicare payments were about to be cut off. They wanted to transfer her to a nursing home, even though she still needed hospitalization.

Janet fought back and fought back hard. She had the whole system from the hospital to the court reeling, backpedaling. Even Ms Rudy got her few minutes of fame, I mean shame, on local television in Rockford.

As I watched Ms Rudy's segment on my computer, she was all decked out and made up and actually smiling. That was something I hadn't seen in the courtroom. But as she spoke, she was vague, not so much talking about the Bedins' case, but saying how tough her job was and that her program was overloaded. She was appointed by the governor and like any politician, she was good at side-stepping the issue at hand.

Going back to the written article on this site, I read how public guardians wrestle the rights of senior citizens away from them and drain their savings. The article went on to explain how guardians also have the ability to sell their homes to collect their fees. This should be criminal.

When all was said and done, Janet Bedin had what I saw as a hollow victory. Ms Rudy didn't get guardianship. Janet was able to bring her mother home and spend what little time Delores had left with her. However, for whatever reason, to protect the courts, Ms Rudy, whomever, the court case was sealed and a gag order put in place. Ms Bedin was denied the opportunity to tell the whole story.

But something good came out of Janet Bedin's fight. She was appointed an elder rights liaison to the Illinois legislative branch of the government. Congratulations and thank you, Janet Bedin, for exposing and sharing what you could of your experience, even though you couldn't tell the full story. Not to worry, 'cause I can. You go girl, wow!

A couple of days later, I was still floating high, almost

gloating, at these new discoveries while I drove Mom and Deb down valley to Glenwood Springs to do a follow up visit with Dr. Wiley, Mom's psychiatrist. We all shuffled into his exam room, and as Deb and I watched, he administered the mini-dementia test. Mom's last score of ten out of thirty exercises wasn't so good, but this time, to our disbelief, she scored twenty-eight out of thirty, the same score that Bruce Person had gotten almost two years earlier in March and again in July of 2009. Kim Timmerwilke had been oh, so wrong in her disagreement with Bruce Person, and he was vindicated.

Now I had more than a few questions for the doc. I first asked how in the world Mom had gotten so low to the point that she had to go through the ordeal of medical delirium. He explained the best he could in layman terms that after surgery, even in hospitals he's been associated with, if a person is agitated, it's easier to medicate, which takes about five minutes, than to spend whatever time necessary to get to the bottom of the real problem. A lot of times, this was due to understaffing, and sometimes just to make their jobs easier.

As to Mom's recovery, it was likely due to her being off of antipsychotic or psychotropic drugs that made her cognitive level increase one hundred and fifty percent. The Aricept seemed to work also.

When asked, Dr. Wiley further stated that it was possible that having Deb as her fulltime friend had changed her brain chemistry enough for her to achieve a higher level of functioning. This was so pleasing to hear. We all thanked Dr. Wiley and were on our way. Mom was now functioning better than over half the population, and except for the fact that she'd been adjudicated by the courts in Rockford, she could probably live on her own with simple powers of attorney to help her out. Thank you Dr. Wiley.

Back at the metal cabin on the river, it was spring of

2011 as I finished up my writing. I was on the computer again, when I typed Ms Rudy's name into the computer and, yes, once again a new site popped up. Ms Rudy was to be a main speaker at a major elder rights conference in Chicago. She was to speak on the duties of a guardian ad litem. Maybe she'd be better off teaching how to manipulate the courts and to have your cases sealed, for her privacy, not yours.

As I read about the conference, I saw that it was made up of lawyers and advocates on both sides of elder rights. There were lawyers who sue nursing homes and those who defend them, government agencies, you name it. With their dinner cruises and mixers, this group is a little too tight knit for my liking. I'd like to think that they'd do more than give the issues lip service, but I don't know.

As for Ms Rudy, I'd like to thank Janet Bedin again for standing her up so I could knock her down. This isn't personal; this is business. Borrowing a quote from my local paper, The Aspen Daily News, "If you don't want it printed, don't let it happen." This court jester won't be kicked around anymore. I only hope my book enlightens people to take notice and come to action. Power to the people!

CHAPTER XXVII
HERE'S THE DEAL

So here's the deal. My story is most likely one of thousands, and Rockford, Illinois, and the 17th Judicial District Court are just a small speck on the map. As I write, cases of elderly abuse are still happening every day, and most of them are going unreported across our country. The players in my cautionary tale could have remained unnamed, but every time I found it hard to write the next word, I threw caution to the wind. I wanted the truth to be known.

We all have rights as US citizens. However, as this population of boomers hits the wall of aging minds and bodies, our rights are being violated. We live in a country that was set up on the premise that no one, man or woman, should fear another. But that's not the way it is. Even though Janet Bedin's case and mine couldn't be any more different, they both boiled down to who has the rights. The right to an attorney, to due process of law, and to present evidence. The court in my case took it all away, off the table. Mom's rights didn't matter and Janet Bedin fought for her mother and won. But they sealed the case so there was no transparency. Follow the money. Money, money, your money. If and when they do adjudicate you or someone you love, it's almost impossible to reverse. They take your rights and you are left with fewer rights than a prisoner on death row.

Then there's big pharma and the private nursing

home Gulag. The drug manufacturers play the odds. They expect to pay fines; they know they're committing crimes with their kick-back schemes. For them, it's the cost of doing business. In the scam involving Omnicare and Johnson and Johnson, they made 20 billion dollars or more and were only fined 2 billion, or ten percent, in the same time period. I'm sure they'll pay only a fraction of that amount. That's good business, but at the expense of our health. Part of that fine was a criminal penalty, but no one went to jail; it's just money.

The nursing home Gulag is much worse. They medicate to death because they're understaffed and/or are lazy and just don't care about the patients. It's maximum profit and minimum care. Medicaid pays an average of $75,000 a year per person, double occupancy. People, we're standing in a puddle and don't even know our feet are wet. How much of this are we willing to take?

There was one case in Illinois where a doctor went to prison for six years for offering money to homeless people to go to nursing homes. He wanted to fill beds so the nursing homes could bilk Medicare and Medicaid for millions, and he could get his kickbacks. This has got to stop.

Alden Village North, a nursing home for the developmentally disabled, was finally shut down after too many children died. They were given a $50,000 fine, but they ended up paying less than thirty percent of it.

I've seen other Medicaid scams. My mother needs pull-ups at night, adult diapers, so through a private agency we now receive them. But here's the hitch. They don't work. It takes three pair to do what store-bought Depends do, and who knows how much they're billing the government. And it's our money.

Then when Mom's Medicaid was going to be terminated,

the case worker gave me a choice of two devices. One was an "I've Fallen Down, and I Can't Get Up" pendant for Mom to use to call in the troops if something happened to her. The other choice was a Med-Ready automatic pill dispenser that was cheaply made and cost about $150 retail. It had an alarm to remind dementia patients to take their pills. I thought to myself that if they were so bad off, and my mother wasn't, they'd probably forget what the alarm was for.

I decided on the Med Ready to keep her Medicaid in force so I wouldn't have to go through the juggernaut of reapplying, since they'd messed it up that first time. While Mom was at the senior center, a man came and delivered it and gave me a fifteen minute presentation and also a parts list, which meant I'd have to repair it if it broke.

When I met with Mom's case worker, I told her what choice I'd made, and then asked how much the government was paying for it. She replied that it cost $62.50. I stated that they cost more than that retail. She looked at me and said, "Sixty-two fifty a month." My jaw hit the floor. That's seven hundred plus a year, and they don't do any follow up service. I wondered to myself how many units the government is paying for, 100,000, possibly a million. Do the math. It could be costing us upwards of half a billion dollars. That's a scam, and we're all paying for it.

This is casual corruption, as I call it, and it's running rampant through our society, from the Wall Street failure to the defense department to our healthcare system, for the elderly as well as the rest of us. It's ripping the very fabric of our society to pieces, and we're like lemmings, just walking into the sea.

What we do is flip on the TV and watch for weeks on end, the Tiger Wood saga and the Charlie Sheen circus that I was so close to with only one degree of separation.

What we don't do is hold our media responsible. This corruption of our courts and healthcare system should be headline news, not buried in the paper on page four, or just occasionally on national news. This is going to be a national epidemic. Are we that numb or over-medicated, or do we just not care? I don't know. Are we waiting for it to collapse? We've seen Mickey Rooney go before congress and plead. Does it just fall on deaf ears, or do they just give lip service to pacify us? Our country consumes 75% of all drugs made for mental illness in the world. It has to stop somewhere before we're all medicated to death.

I've come up with some of my own ideas to help in this battle. In a family court situation, go pro se. If enough people do this, it would clog up the courts and wreak havoc on the system until they'd have to make changes. Practice non-violent civil disobedience. Protest at court houses and nursing homes so the media will get the message out. The life you're saving may be your own.

You can also write to your senator or congressman, both at the state and federal levels. You can even write to your president. This is not a Democratic or Republican issue; this is an American issue. Where there's power, there's corruption. Let them know you're watching. Go to the library, go online, do your own research. Check out the National Association to Stop Guardianship Abuse. Google "Growing trends in medicine" or The Miami Herald's "Neglected to Death." You'll see for yourself.

You could also join or start watchdog groups, stir the shit storm. Maybe, just maybe, you could cause one of these dominoes of corruption to fall, causing a chain reaction. Do this before it's too late and we have the largest unnatural disaster, both morally and financially, this country has ever seen.

I, myself, have other ideas, such as communal senior

living communities and required staffing at nursing facilities. Nursing homes need to be brought out of the archaic time of yesteryear where they were run like sanitariums or asylums. Do volunteer work. Play music. Do art for or with them, or simply just be a friend. Otherwise, we might as well just stone our elders to death. It would probably be more humane. And let the lawyers and judges who helped cause this mayhem cast the first stone.

Think about it. If we required the nursing homes to staff properly with RN's, CNA's and other health care professionals, we could probably reduce unemployment in this country by one percent or more. We need to think outside the box and be proactive, not reactive.

Nothing you do in your life will be this important for the freedom of others or yourself. It's your decision; it's up to you. If we're not put on this planet to help each other, then what are we put here for? Think about it.

And as for Mom, her situation is no longer precarious. She's happy, and when my editor Joy saw her for the first time in a couple of months, she couldn't believe it. Joy had been in contact with Mom from day one; she helped Mom out. Now, as she watched my mother in her full grace, painting, happy, relaxing without fear, the look on her face was so rewarding. I just can't find the right word to describe my mom's recovery. I guess I could use "miracle." I can only hope that my book does well enough to carry her home.

As for the skull, the last time I talked to Randy from the FBI was almost a year ago. He was in Egypt just before the revolution and couldn't talk. I thought that was a strange place for an agent to be vacationing. I didn't need to know why he was there and didn't ask. He told me, however, that he'd call me when he returned stateside. I said, "No hurry, no worries." I think I'll hear from him soon. Nor have I called Mike Arians, the man from Oregon, Illinois, with the investigation of the double homicide in 1948 where Mary Jane Reed's skull was missing. I just haven't had the time.

All I do know is that on that rainy wet day, when I was nine years old, under the front porch of our family home so long ago, I held the skull in my hand!

"Fiat justita ruat caelum" *

* Let justice be done though the heavens fall

EPILOGUE

There's many a slip between a cup and a lip or a self-fulfilling prophecy, call it what you will; a lot has gone down since my book was finished, with the last entries made in January, 2011, and the final editing before publishing done in June.

Every month since March, Ms Rudy has sent me her bill for $3,600 marked "Past Due" in bright red ink. There was also one on April 1, 2011, for $7,000 along with a note telling me to quit sending Mom's medically related bills to her. Mom's bills were to be paid by my father through her office as part of the court order. The court order also laid out the timetable I was to use to pay her, which was after I paid Ms Timmerwilke's bill off at $50 a month. Did her ears fall off? I thought this was some sort of April Fool's joke.

As for Ms Timmerwilke, she also sent me a letter in late spring of 2011. I hadn't heard from her since December, 2010, when my father had gone to the hospital in serious condition. That's when I asked if I could put Mom back in her home. The letter, however, was for a name change to McKenzie. She stated she'd call me in a few days to explain. I thought that would be a good time to ask her once again that if my father wasn't in their marital home, could I bring Mom back. But that call never came. So her checks continued to be sent made out to Kim Timmerwilke.

I didn't bother to call her since I was too busy finishing my book. When the final manuscript was completed, I had it put into book form and sent several copies out to different news and government agencies: The Chicago Tribune, The L.A. Times, WIFR Television Station in Rockford, The Diane Rehm Show, and possibly Oprah, the attorney general's and the governor's offices in Illinois, and I also sent one to President Obama.

At about this time in late July, 2011, the self-fulfilling prophecy happened. I received a motion from the courts to sell Mom's house to pay for their legal fees. At this point I'm thoroughly disgusted. I thought I'd made it clear to Ms Timmerwilke that my Mother's only wish was to be back in her own home. Then it dawned on me. During the course of those court hearings, I had asked Kim if Mom should get divorced. She stated that if Mom stayed married and Dad were to die, Mom would get everything. Looking back now, I guess we were playing a game of "Texas Hold'em." I'd been had.

For the next three days I attempted to contact Attorney Timmerwilke with two phone calls and an email. While I was at the computer doing more research, I punched in Janet Bedin's name again, and voila, much to my surprise and sadness, Janet's mother Dolores had passed. God bless her soul. She'd fought the good fight. So I went to the obits online and gave my condolences and my contact number. I thought maybe I'd get to talk with Janet personally, even though I felt I already knew her in an odd way.

Mom's ad litem and her advocate Ms Timmerwilke called three days later. I told her I received the motion on August 30, one day after the hearing. She stated that she didn't believe me. Then I asked why she didn't call, and she said the mailing was sufficient notice. She knew that throughout my mother's case there have been more than a few times when court was cancelled or moved without my being notified until it was too late. I just didn't understand. I guess another formality.

As we continued our conversation I informed Kim that the proof of service wasn't dated, only notarized, and that Ms Rudy stated that I wasn't paying them according to court orders. Kim assured me that she'd let her know I was. I then let her know of Ms Rudy's other misstatements. Except for the fact that the motion's first point was to make my father qualify for long-term care, the rest of the motion was for payment of their legal fees. It also stated that they could sell Mom's home at 75% of the appraised value. Then it dawned on me. A federal law I'd read during my research stated that if the estate is worth less than $100,000, one spouse can't leave the other homeless if they go into a nursing facility. Then I remembered that early on in court they appraised the estate at $101,000, not $99,000. How convenient. Another coup d'état. Not only have they left my mother indigent and toothless, they apparently want to leave her homeless as well. Bad form.

As our conversation came to an end, Kim told me my only option was to file a motion to dismiss due to insufficient notice. I thanked her before hanging up, but I didn't know what for.

If this motion became a court order, they would sell the house to pay for what amounted to $10,000 in legal fees, about fifty hours of legal work at $200 an hour. This would also provide money for the realtor, appraiser, and other fees they may incur. After splitting the proceeds with my father, I think there would only be enough money to bury Mom.

Back on the computer and with the help of Arthur, we create a "motion to dismiss." I'm back in court. Yuck! I accomplished this with the help of Fed Ex and my brother Bill. It was filed within five days with hand delivered service to appropriate parties and the court.

Enter Janet Bedin again. After numerous calls to television station Channel 23 in Rockford, I finally made contact with reporter Tina Stein. She had just received my manuscript from her news director. Tina had done the three part series "Growing Trends in Medicine: The Dolores Bedin Story." She was very interested in what I had to say since Janet is the subject of my final chapters. She asked if I would do a TV interview when I was back in Rockford. I told her I'd be glad to, but I didn't have a court date yet. Before we hung up, I asked if she would give me Ms Bedin's email address, and she said "yes." She said Janet would probably be delighted to hear from me since we were in similar situations with the courts. I thanked her and emailed Janet immediately.

It only took a day and Janet Bedin called and left a message on my phone. We finally connected. After extending my condolences to Janet and her family, we exchanged stories. There were a lot of similarities in what we'd both gone through with Ms Rudy and the courts. After many phone calls and emails, we became comrades at arms, working for the same cause. We both felt that this will be a long and productive relationship.

Janet showed me what court documents she could due to the gag order in her case and later testimonial letters from Governor Thompson and other politicians she works for. She also showed me one from her ex-fiancé who works for the US Attorney's office in Rockford. In his letter he made Janet sound like the angel that she is. He stated that she helped him through the death of his mother and other trials and tribulations, and that she was now an advocate for victims of guardianship abuse in Illinois. He also wrote that their break-up was no fault of hers and was due to his own personal issues. After reading it, I couldn't believe that he'd let a woman like this go and dismiss her as her mother was dying. So after I finished reading his letter, I called Janet.

Talking with Janet, I told her that the letter from her ex was beautifully written, and that I couldn't understand how her fiancé could leave her at a time like that, or at all for that matter. There was a long pause on the phone; then, as she spoke, her voice cracked. Apparently, during her mother's illness, her ex had taken a lover. He went over the fence, and to my shock and dismay, the other woman was Ms Kim Timmerwilke. Things started to make sense. I'd gone to the US Attorney's Office, which is next to Kim's, twice, only to be turned away. They didn't want to hear my case. More collusion? I don't know.

As Janet spoke, almost crying, she said that on her final court date, when she walked into court, she saw Ms Timmerwilke showing off her engagement ring to Ms Rudy. I thought to myself that through their indiscretion, Kim and Janet's ex had shown what little integrity and honesty they have. As I consoled Janet, she went on to say how hard this had been to go it alone and that I was lucky to still have a mother. I agreed. Later, through public records, I discovered that the new Mrs. McKenzie and Janet's ex had purchased the house next door to Judge Fabiano's father. And I didn't think that things could get any weirder.

As I finished this epilogue, I received the court order of September 1 on the 10th of September granting all the motions, though flawed. I called Kim, but I don't expect to hear from her. As I file a motion to vacate order with the deck stacked against me, my final thought is I only hope I get a break.

J.H.W.

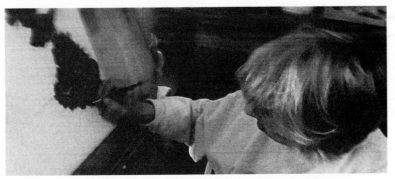

"It's a great life if you don't weaken." (John Buchan)

Two years ago, John Wyman's mother, Carol, walked out of a nursing home in Rockford, Illinois. She had been placed there for the convenience of others, not for her own well-being, and had suffered mentally, physically, and emotionally. When she ended up at John's trailer outside of Aspen, Colorado, his journey began.

Hairdresser by trade, rebel at heart, John took on the challenge of dealing with nursing homes, courts, and family members to provide the best possible situation for his mother. What he experienced woke him up to the inequities and injustices lurking in the systems which have been established to help our older population. He decided to share his story to make us all aware of the catastrophic possibilities that lie in wait if we don't take action to change these systems.

John's book, an autobiographical cautionary tale, is timely and relevant to anyone who may someday become old. With candor, pathos, and humor, John describes his many trips between Aspen and Rockford, providing the reader with priceless peeks into these two very different worlds. Through his experiences and his research, John has learned that our aging population has become a lucrative source of profits for unscrupulous organizations and individuals. His purpose in writing this book is to alert the rest of us to this dire situation in hopes that we will wake up and act.

John Howard Wyman was born in 1955 in Rockford, Illinois. He spent the last thirty years living in the Aspen area. He is an award winning, world renowned hairdresser whose clients have included world politicians and celebrities. An accomplished ceramic artist, he has collaborated with two internationally recognized artists. This is his first book.